Maidy

June Houghton Gatewood

authorHOUSE°

uthorHouse™
1663 Liberty Drive
Bloomington, IN 47403
www.authorhouse.com
Phone: 833-262-8899

Published by AuthorHouse   10/10/2023

ISBN: 979-8-8230-0840-2 (sc)
ISBN: 979-8-8230-0841-9 (hc)
ISBN: 979-8-8230-0842-6 (e)

Library of Congress Control Number: 2023908961

Print information available on the last page.

Contents

Dedication

I would like to dedicate this book to my three children, Suzy, Donna and James. You have supported and loved me through my long journey of writing this book. It has taken ten years to finish this project, and without your love and patience, it would have not been possible. A special thank you to my son for assisting me with copyediting this text. I would also like to thank the many friends and writers who have shared their thoughts about this book and helped to make it a stronger text including my friend, Kevin, the Museum of Tolerance writer's group and my writer's group in the Bay Area.

I have written about the many trials and tribulations I experienced during my childhood, experiences which I covered with mental bandages in later years. Through the process of writing this book, I was able to remove them one by one until I finished the last page of my story. I feel proud I had the courage and conviction to live my life, bending it to my true self, knowing that only I had the power through God to change my life.

Through you three children and by beautiful grandchildren, I learned to love and be loved.

Through God all things are possible

Thank you.

Your British Mum

Chapter 1

Suffer Little Children
Come Unto Thee

Devon is a seaside resort surrounded by rocky cliffs and sandy shores. It is known as the crown jewel of the English Riviera with a comparatively mild climate that draws visitors from across the kingdom. Its coastline and landscape make Devon a destination for recreation and leisure. Visitors come from all over the United Kingdom and abroad to visit, but in 1940 it was a place for refugee children escaping from the horrors of war.

This is where my story begins.

It was a cold wet day in October 1942, when my sister, Jeanette and I arrived at an orphanage accompanied by our mother and her sister, Aunt Ruby. A black taxi had dropped us off in front of a large stone building, the Priory Convent of Marychurch with the few meager possessions Jeanette and I possessed. We stood frozen in front of the large wooden doors. My body was pressed so tightly against my sister that there was almost one person standing on the front doorstep.

I started to cry and rubbed my eyes on my sister's wool skirt. Jeanette bent down and said, "Don't cry Maidy. We must be brave."

Maidy was a nickname my father gave to me because I loved playing with the dustpan and brush, but my birth name is June.

I looked up at my mother, but she avoided my gaze, staring ahead and pressing the doorbell, waiting for someone to answer as she wiped tears from her eyes, not knowing what was about to happen would change all our lives from that day forth.

I was born in a country engulfed in war, where sirens blared defiantly over the loud roar of German aircrafts dropping bombs over England. We were terrified as we had no idea why we were here at Marychurch. Jeanette was holding my hand so tight. It hurt me! I felt sick and I wanted to pee but where would I pee?

A loud rap at the front door by my mother was answered by a nun with a large chain of wooden beads flapping across her habit.

"Sister Catherine Angela," my mother said, "These are my daughters, the girls, I spoke to you about during our meeting last week."

"Hello," Sister Catherine Angelcs said, peering over the metal rims of her glasses. From where I stood, she appeared as an older large woman, with a round face on a short neck. When she smiled her face lit up with kindness. She wore a wide stiff white collar, neatly starched over her black habit, giving her the appearance of a huge penguin. Leaning down to look us over, she nodded in approval. Then she looked at Aunty Ruby and Mummy and said, "You can leave the girls here with me. We will take good care of them. Girls, say goodbye to your mother and aunt."

"Goodbye, Mummy," Jeanette said, trying to hold back the tears.

Mummy then looked at me and said, "Goodbye, Maidy."

I let out a piercing scream. "Mummy, Mummy, don't leave me!"

She bent down and patted my head saying, "I will be back soon."

We both gave my mother a quick hug and cried watching her walk out the big wooden door, still wiping tears from her eyes as Aunty Ruby wrapped her arm around her waist to support her. It would be a long time before we would see her again.

Jeanette grabbed my hand, and we both followed Sister Catherine Angela into the convent. We entered a dimly lit hall, extending the entire length of the building. The strong smell of carbolic soap filled the air. Jeanette and I were scared of our new surroundings.

"Who are all these women dressed like penguins wearing a cross around their neck?" I thought as I took in my surroundings.

Too much was happening, and I didn't understand. I squeezed my sister's hand so tightly she let out a yell. At that very moment all the air in my tiny lungs was set free. Sister Catherine Angeles turned around and looked at us with a big smile on her red face. "Welcome to Marychurch, girls. This will be your new home until your mother returns."

Jeanette spoke in a low voice, "Sister, how long will Mummy leave us here?"

Sister looked down with that same smile on her face and said, "God has sent you to us until Mummy is able to take you."

Jeanette was puzzled. "Who is God?" she asked.

"God made you and Maidy and gave you both as a gift to your mother and father. He created you and the world we live in. You will learn many wonderful things about his son Jesus and his parents. You will visit his church and learn how to say prayers," Sister replied.

Jeanette grabbed my hand, and we continued to follow Sister down the hallway until it gave way to a brightly lit room with long oak wooden tables. Seated at the tables quietly eating were rows of girls of all different ages. All eyes shifted our way while Jeanette and I stood leaning on each other. They were eating spaghetti from blue china bowls. The smell of the food was delicious, but all I could do was hang on to my sister. We both were shaking with fear.

A chorus of whispering voices fill the air. We both jumped as a thundering noise erupted above our heads. Sister Catherine Angela had clapped her hands several times to dispel the noise.

"Silence girls! Silence! We have two new girls joining us today. This is Maidy and Jeanette. They are from Plymouth. Please welcome them to Marychurch."

We heard chairs scraping against the dull linoleum floors

and the once-seated girls were now on their feet, moving towards us in a slow silent rush.

"Welcome to Marychurch," a girl with orange hair said, offering her hand to my sister.

"Welcome," said another girl whose glasses were too big for her face. She looked down at me and said, "You're too young to live here."

My sister looked right at her and said, "No she is not, and she is going to stay here with me."

"Hello," said a girl with black pigtails. "My name is Shirley, and I'm from London."

So many girls crowded around us, and Sister Catherine Angela knew that we were overwhelmed. She stood between us and commanded the children to go back to their seats.

Over time Jeanette learned why we were in the orphanage.

"Maidy, we're here because Daddy is dead and Mummy doesn't want us anymore," she told me one night before bed.

My daddy, whom I adored and and who nicknamed me Maidy because I loved playing with the dustpan and brush, was gone, and so was my Mummy.

This was our new world, our new home, and Jeannette and I were both scared for our future.

Ten years would pass before my mother took me home.

Shortly after our arrival at Marychurch, Jeanette and I were baptized Catholics with our mother's permission. This was done in Our Lady Help of Christians and St Denis church during the Sunday mass. Two novice nuns stood up for Jeanette and me as our godmothers. Mine was Sister Teresa, who lifted me up to a white stone basin. I can remember holy water being poured over my head and the priest saying, "I baptize you. In the name of the Father, Son and Holy Ghost."

Starting school at five years old, I attended mass each morning before breakfast. Sister Teresa taught me to pray on the rosary by holding onto a small crucifix with beads arranged in a circle attached to the cross. I found it difficult to recite the long prayers they expected us to know by heart, but she explained the rosary is a special way of praying.

Sister Teresa said, "Maidy, When you say the prayers of the rosary in church with the priest, think about Jesus. Think about the bible stories you hear at mass on Sunday. As you grow older, you will learn to say the rosary on your own, and make friends with Jesus, someone to trust, and talk to."

During my early years I did not understand the full consequences of war, but I can remember the great care with which the Catholic nuns took care of us in the orphanage. They fed me, dressed me, and comforted me when I cried. As I look back and try to get a clear memory of the nuns, I think of their endearing faces and caring hands when I was sick with my colds, measles, and chicken pox.

Through their teaching I learned compassion, trust and humility at a very young age. The nuns introduced me to God and the Holy Bible through the Catholic religion, which gave me the strength and fortitude to understand my family relationships, and gave me a spiritual connection with my dead father which has comforted me throughout my life.

Chapter 2

My Holy Family

I lived with many refugees from Europe who were escaping from the terror of war, but we blended as one group, wearing blue uniform dresses and sharing a common sense of loss. Loss of our parents and the pain of rejection.

On Saturday mornings, the nuns gave us warm baths in gray metal tubs with large rings hanging from each end. After I stepped out of the bathtub, a nun would dry me with a large white towel that felt like a hairbrush on my skin. It smelt like country air from hanging on the washing line in the garden. After they dried my body, they gave me clean underwear and socks.

I can still see the blue cotton knickers in large piles on the long wooden table stacked neatly by a brown wicker basket full of white socks. The white undervests were sitting in a neat pile next to the knickers. The nuns laid the blue cotton dresses across another table in different sizes. In the winter we had warm blue knitted cardigans, which were worn over our dresses.

I hated having my hair washed by the nuns as they hurt me when they squeezed my hair in a knot to get the excess water out, before passing me to a novice nun to rub it dry with another white rough towel from the clothesline.

There were two girls in front of me that cried each time

they had their hair washed, and I said, in a hushed voice to the one named Betty, "You're a big baby."

Mary, her friend, who was also crying, said, "Shut up Maidy!"

"Who's going to make me?" I shouted.

Suddenly, I heard Sister Oliver's voice speaking. "Hush," She said.

She was standing close by and looked at us with a big frown on her face. She wore that frown quite often and did not have patience for confrontations between us girls.

Sister Oliver was round around the middle and reminded me of a plum pudding with custard on her head. She was one nun you did not want to upset. One look from sister said a thousand words. Whenever I was close to her I started to fidget with my feet tapping up and down.

"Maidy, stand still and stop fidgeting," she said.

I dreaded my haircuts, which were every two months. Sister Oliver would place a basin on my head, and cut my hair around it. My new friend, Shirley, whom I met in the first year of school, was a refugee from London, and she said, "This is the monk's haircut."

Ellen, my other friend, who liked to play hide-and –seek with me said, "What is a Monk?

"I don't know," I said.

Joan, who was standing in line behind Shirley giggled and suddenly burst out, "A monk is a monkey and lives at the zoo."

I looked straight at her and said, "You look like a monkey with long arms."

She started to cry and Sister Oliver gave me a nasty look, and then threatened me with a slap with the ruler. She made me apologize to Joan immediately, and I sulked for the rest of the day.

Once a month we had our nails cut. I can remember the nun giving me a slap on my hands as I bit my fingernails almost to the quick.

"This is a nasty habit, Maidy. You pray to the blessed Virgin Mary to help you busy your mind through reading the bible," Sister Catherine said.

After our baths the dirty laundry was put in a white cart on wheels, and taken to the laundry room by the postulant nuns. It was washed by hand in a big gray metal tub by the nuns, and rung through two wooden rolls that looked like rolling pins connected to a big metal wheel and a wooden handle. The nuns called it a mangle machine. The machine squeezed out excess water before the clothes and sheets were hung on the washing line with wooden pegs to secure them. Ten long washing lines were hooked on to metal poles and long wooden sticks were used to hoist up the washing. The lines were located on the right side of the convent.

When it was a windy day, the sheets and pillowcases looked like parachutes blowing up and down, and they made loud squeaky sounds against the washing lines. I could see them from my dormitory window. On a rainy day, my friends and I would watch the nuns run outside and take the washing off the line. If any laundry fell on the ground, we would squeal with laughter.

Ellen, my friend from London, would sing, "Rain, rain go away, come back another day." Then we would all chime in with the song.

When I was five years old, I went to school with girls who lived outside the orphanage in the village. They were called the "outdoor girls" and we were called the "indoor girls."

During the day I attended school from 8:00 am until 4:00pm. Tea was served at 4:30pm. At 6:00pm the day would end with us going to church for Benediction and saying the rosary. The rosary is a chain of beads, which represent prayers. It has five decades of beads consisting of Our Father, the Gloria, and ten Hail Mary to one decade.

The benediction was the longest service I attended, and the priest spoke it in Latin, a language which I was studying in school. I sat on a long oak wooden bench in church and was constantly sucking on the rosary beads. They tasted like nothing. As I grew older with thoughts of becoming a nun, the rosary became my greatest solace. I would pray on it often, asking for help. It continues to be an important part of my life to this day. As a child, I could not see Jesus, but I felt Him in my heart. I knew he was close by. Something drew me to Jesus, the Son of God, through a deep love and compassion from my inner soul. I believed he was my connection and inner strength to life.

As I look back on my childhood, I remember that I almost did not make my First Communion, which was a special event. A commitment to the body and blood of Jesus Christ, which you receive at Mass in the form of bread and wine. I was seven years old and had demolished a row of beads from my rosary. The beads were made from raw dried beans. Looking at my beads I said, "My God, what have I done?"

I was scared! I had completely chewed the beans off the rosary chain. I did this in church during service as I was worried I would wet my knickers if I couldn't get to the bathroom in time. I needed to go twice during mass, but the sister in charge would let me go only one time.

Before we made our communion, we gathered together as a group in church to practice walking down the aisle preparing to receive the sacrament of Holy Communion. Sister Catherine ordered us to wear our rosary beads around our necks.

As I walked by Sister Catherine Angela, the Mother Superior, she saw my half hung rosary dangling around my neck. She looked horrified as she marched over to me with a scowl on her face, and pulled me out of the line. Through clenched teeth she said, to the other children in a loud voice,

"Maidy has eaten the Hail Mary beads and should not make her first Holy Communion."

I started to shake and wished I could have fainted right there in the aisle.

Sister said, "Maidy get on your knees and say an act of contrition."

I knelt down on the cold stone floor and prayed to God to forgive me for chewing the rosary beads. I sobbed as my heart was aching for hurting the Hail Mary beads, and I knew Jesus was upset with me because Mary was his mother. I stayed on my knees until our group left the church.

Sister Catherine came towards me and said, "You should be ashamed of yourself Maidy. Get off your knees and go to the dining room for tea."

That night I punished myself by putting my legs up on the cold wall for one hour, praying for Jesus to forgive me. Eventually I cried myself to sleep. The next day I went to find Sister Teresa. She was in the library and I ran to her and said, "Mother Superior will not let me make my Communion."

She looked at me and said, "I will talk to you later, Maidy. I am busy looking for a book."

At lunchtime Sister Teresa saw me from across the room and walked over to my table and in a low voice said, "Maidy, Mother Superior spoke to me regarding you chewing your rosary beads, and told me you will not be making your first communion. Why did you chew the beads off your holy rosary?" she asked.

With tears brimming in my eyes I said, "I was hungry. I am sorry Sister Teresa, but I want to make my communion with my friends, and I promise I will not chew the beads again."

Sister looked at me sadly and said, "I will speak to Sister Catherine, and tell her how sorry you are, and if you stop crying, I will see if I can get you another rosary."

I waited to hear back from her. After two agonizing days I was finally called from my classroom to Sister Catherine's office.

I went to find my sister Jeanette in her classroom. I stood at the door shaking. She was in study hall without her teacher. I opened the door and called out her name. She looked up from her study book and came towards me and said, "Maidy, Is everything alright?"

I replied, "I need you to go with me to Sister Catherine's office. She wants to see me about the rosary, and I am so scared."

Jeanette said, "Don't worry Maidy, I will come with you."

Before we entered the office, I peeked through the glass window and was glad to see Sister Teresa speaking with Mother Superior who was sitting in her leather brown chair behind her desk. When she heard us knock on the door, she waved her hand for us to enter her office.

She looked up from her desk with a grim look on her reddish face. There were wisps of gray hair sticking out from her head veil. Her body looked like a man's shoe, she was tall like a tree, and was old enough to be my grandmother.

Yes, I was scared of her.

"Good afternoon girls," she said. "Maidy, stand in front of my desk, and Jeanette you sit on the chair here."

She stared at me, and my whole body was shaking. I felt I had committed a mortal sin and did not deserve to make my Holy Communion. She looked directly at me and said, "After discussing the subject of the rosary beads with Sister Teresa, we have decided you will be given another chance to make your Holy Communion. Sister Teresa will give you another rosary, and it will be checked weekly to see whether you have broken the nasty habit of chewing the beads. Your penance is to recite one rosary by kneeling beside your bed before going to sleep for one week."

I thanked both the nuns and said, "I am very sorry and will never chew on my rosary again."

I saw a half smile on Sister Teresa's face, but Mother Superior's face remained grim.

We left the office. My sister hugged me and said, "Maidy, chew on your fingernails, not the beads."

"I can't chew my nails or I will get a slap from the bath nun," I said.

We both laughed out loud, and walked back to our classrooms, hand in hand.

The next day after morning mass Sister Teresa gave me my new rosary. It was beautiful. It was chestnut brown and felt smooth as silk to touch. I thanked her and promised her that I would take good care of it. I ran to find my best friends Shirley and Ellen to show them my new rosary.

"We can all make our communion together," Shirley said.

The three of us walked in the back garden towards the rose bushes because I told them I wanted to bury my old rosary under the rose bush and it would be our secret. Ellen reached down and picked up a stone and dug a hole under the yellow roses.

"Ow!" Ellen yelled, "I pricked myself from the thorn of the rose."

"Look, there is blood on your finger," said Shirley.

Maidy looked at Shirley and said, "We have to prick our finger and rub our blood on the rosary. This will make us blood sisters until we die."

We pricked our fingers with a loud yelp, and smeared the rosary with our blood and laid the old rosary on the ground.

Placing our hands on the rosary, we bent down and each kissed the crucifix and looked at each other and said, "We are blood sisters until death do we part."

We put the rosary in the newly dug hole and Shirley covered it with gravel. We spread rose petals around the area.

"This will be our special place to pray, and we will come here when we are sad and need some love from Jesus," I said.

I looked up to the sky and could see the clouds snuggling together. This meant the rain was coming. The first drops began to fall and we started to run and skip back to the convent, our home.

Chapter 3

Our Lady of Christians and St. Denis

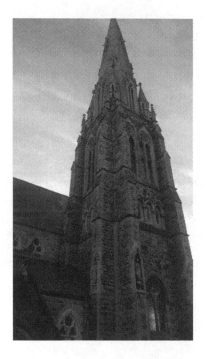

Our Lady of Christians and St. Denis was the Catholic Church that adjoined the Marychurch orphanage. I visited daily, struck by the breathtaking architecture. The church was magnificent, inside and out.

The priest spent time with us to explain to us the history of the church, which began in the nineteenth century. The

Saxon monks carried the first large stones to the top of the hill where the first small church was built and erected. In the spring of 1864, the Bishop of Plymouth invited Mother Margaret Hallahan and her Dominican nuns to find a house in some parts of his diocese. Mother Margaret proposed a suitable establishment for an orphanage and school for girls in the village of Marychurch in South Devon.

When Mother Margaret first visited Marychurch, all that remained of the original church was an ancient tower. Mother Margaret came away from the church saying: "It is very handsome, but I will build Our Lady a better church." She had no idea then how it was to be accomplished, but the magnificent church was completed by the end of the nineteenth century.

The order had many young women, novices who were training to become full-fledged nuns. It was the home of the Holy Dominican order. One of the exits in the church went downstairs to the cloisters where the nuns prayed. When we were in Benediction, this was the entrance that the novices came into the church, and it was forbidden territory. The only time children were permitted to enter the cloisters was if they needed to go to the bathroom, and the nuns only allowed us to go once during mass.

On one occasion I had to go to the bathroom twice during Sunday Mass, and Sister Mary blocked me from going.

She whispered in my ear, "If you get up one more time, there will be consequences."

I was so nervous that I ended up wetting my knickers and leaving a small puddle on the bench. I told no one and never heard any word regarding my misfortune.

Each time I come home to England, I visit Marychurch. I catch the number eighty-five red double decker bus from Exeter to Torquay and take another bus to Priory Road. I can see the church steeple in the distance, and as I walk closer I stop to gaze at this beautiful church. I feel her arms reaching out to me and drawing me through the rugged oak doors.

Nothing seems to have changed. Only the people. This trip, I arrived in time for the morning mass. I knelt down in the pew, made the sign of the cross, and participated in the service.

During the priest's sermon, my eyes wandered around the church, and I observed the same people that I saw in previous years attending mass with a couple of new faces.

I wanted to get up and walk up to the pulpit and introduce myself, saying out loud, "This was my home. I was a war baby, and I grew up here in this church. I am proud of who I am today because of this church, which inspired me, and the nuns that raised me in the orphanage."

But I sat in silence and had a million thoughts running through my mind of my childhood days at Marychurch.

I ran my fingers along the polished oak wooden pew, the same pew I had sat in when I attended Mass and benediction as a little girl. After mass ended, I went to the forbidden door and pushed it open with the force of my hand. I smiled knowing full well that Sister Mary Catherine was no longer there to stop me.

The school and convent are now a retirement home for the Dominican Order of the nuns and priests. As I found my way to the bathroom, I noticed the cloisters were deserted and dusty with cobwebs. Some scattered old books lay on the shelves that lined the hallway. I pushed a big wooden door open and went into the bathroom. The room had a musty smell and seemed so much smaller than I remembered as a child.

When I came out of the bathroom I wandered down the narrow cloisters until I came to a quaint glass solarium where three elderly nuns were sitting on leather wing back chairs. They were surprised to see me.

One of the nuns called out to me, "Can I help you?'

I smiled and said, "No thank you." I waved to the nuns, and they smiled and nodded their heads. I had stumbled into the retirement facility, and the three ladies I had seen were retired nuns.

I stopped in front of a narrow red glass stained window and looked out onto the courtyard. In a flash from my past, it was filled with children laughing and playing hide-and-seek around the maple trees. I see myself bending down, drawing hopscotch squares with a piece of chalk. This was my favorite game. I still see my sister Jeanette, carrying a music sheet to her piano lesson. She looks up and waves at me. I blow her a kiss. Suddenly it was silent and I saw only the trees and rain clouds hovering in the sky.

As I entered back into the church, I bumped into an old priest wearing his garments for Mass "Father, is there another mass today?" I asked.

"Yes," he replied, "in the old chapel around the corner. It will start in five minutes in Latin." I was absolutely thrilled to be able to hear a mass in Latin.

I entered the old Chapel, picked up a worn prayer book located in the pew and sat down by a sweet smiling old lady. I looked around the chapel and could feel the nostalgia in the air. The pews were carved from old cherry wood and had been around for almost a century. There were ten other people in the chapel. Suddenly, everyone stood up and a minister of the church assisted the elderly priest down the aisle. The lady sitting next to me leaned closer and whispered in my ear, "The priest is eighty-five years old and lives at the retirement facility behind the church."

The priest sat down in a Queen Anne chair behind the altar and began the mass in Latin. I was impressed at how articulate he was with the spoken language and surprised at how much I still remembered after all these years.

After mass I spoke to the priest. "Do you remember the orphanage and private school that was once here?" I asked.

He said, "Yes, I came here before it closed, and I know the Dominican nuns did good work with the refugee children from the war."

"I was one of those orphans," I replied, "I now live in the

United States, but I return to England every year and visit Marychurch."

He looked straight at me, and said, "Bless you my child, I pray your life will be at peace."

"Goodbye father, and thank you for the blessing," I said.

I stood outside the church gazing up at a cloudy sky and wondered about inner peace. I have found peace in my later years, but it did not come easily. The struggles of my early childhood have taken a toll on my adult life. I have lived with my raw emotions and anger for many years, feelings that made it difficult for me to find true love or friends, because I was afraid of rejection. I have finally let go and taken a step forward, to set myself free. Through my writing. One page after another, falling in a waterfall around me. This gives me peace and comfort, calming my fears with hope and clarity.

Hearing voices, I suddenly turned and looked at the priest with his caregiver standing close to me near the exit of the church.

"Father, you startled me," I said.

"I am glad you are still here," he said. "I would like to give you a rosary." You will always be welcome at Marychurch. When will you be returning to the United States?"

"In a couple of days," I said. "Thank you for the rosary and the blessing. I needed them both."

Father said, "God bless you my child and have a safe journey."

Chapter 4

Intelligence is the Ability to Adapt to the Rules

After mass I wandered over to the parking area, which was our playground after the war was over. I looked for traces of crayon markings on the ground, but all I could see was a new graveled parking area. I remember the nuns forbidding us to use crayons to draw Hopscotch. It had to be done in white chalk. Mother Superior caught my friends and me using crayons one day, and we had to go to her office.

We stood in front of her desk and she said, "If you girls choose to use crayons instead of white chalk for your hopscotch games, I will not allow you to play in the playground for six months."

She slapped each one of us across the palm of our hands with a stiff wooden ruler, and I can remember it stinging, but all three of us ended up laughing after leaving her office. We continued to use crayons but only when the nuns were in prayer meetings.

Today the parking area is filled with white gravel and light dusty brown dirt where a few cars were parked. I descend down the cobblestone steps leading away from the parking area to check the fruit and vegetable garden. I can see the old greenhouses, one on each side of the garden. I push open a light wooden creaking door and a musty aroma floats in the air.

Someone had filled the greenhouse with garden tools, plant food, potted soil, and brown clay pots of different shapes and sizes. I looked for the old green wheelbarrow, which the nuns used to carry the fruit and vegetables back to the orphanage. It was not there. I checked the other greenhouse, but no wheelbarrow was to be found. Gone too were those big red tomatoes and long green cucumbers we used to eat in our beautiful salads.

I remember the vegetable garden. My friends and I would sit on the steps and watch the novice nuns planting and tending the garden each day. They wore long white veils and white tunic dresses with a black leather belt and long wooden rosary beads attached around the belt. When gardening, they wore long black aprons. The novice nuns received their white habit and black veil when they became a full-fledged nuns. The Dominican nuns wore a black kappa and white habit over their tunic dresses.

"They look like penguins with their black aprons tucked up to their waist when they work," Ellen said one day while all of us watched them while we played.

"They wear long white knickers underneath their dresses," Shirley said. "I've seen them on the washing line."

"They don't wear bras," I chimed in. "I have never seen any on the line."

We giggled and nudged each other.

When the nuns saw us grouped around the steps talking they would say, "Break it up, girls."

We looked at each other and shrugged our shoulders and moved elsewhere.

The garden was my favorite place to spend time with my friends. There were rows and rows of string beans, potatoes, swede, sweet peas, and carrots. The nuns planted cabbages, cauliflower, spinach and marrows in the middle of the garden.

There was red rhubarb planted next to the blackberries and green gooseberries leaning up against an old wooden fence.

During our morning school break, my friends and I would watch two nuns use a wheelbarrow to bring fresh vegetables to the back kitchen door. This was done daily. We were always hungry. Sometimes the nuns would drop some potatoes and carrots. We would pick them up and go behind the churchyard and eat them raw.

Once, the priest caught us laughing and making a commotion. He opened the rectory window and said, "What are you doing out there, girls?"

"Father, we are walking past the church to go back to the classroom," I said.

"I am watching you girls," he said, as he walked back to the rectory.

Shirley said, "You don't think he suspects us of stealing?"

Ellen and I laughed. "Eating food that fell off a wheelbarrow is not stealing," I said.

"Shirley, if you think you are stealing, go to confession on Friday and tell the priest," Ellen said.

"I have nothing to confess," she said.

I remembered at age ten I could work on Saturday mornings in the garden picking out weeds from around the flower beds. Betty Jones was a senior girl in charge of the garden jobs, and she was bossy.

"There will be no talking on the job, and all the weeds in the garden are to be removed and put in the brown rubbish bin behind the greenhouse," she told us during our first orientation. Despite her attitude and all the different rules, working in the garden was such a joy. The soil was rich and reddish in color and it felt good squishing my fingers in it. I would spend time playing in the dirt. I loved running my fingers down the string beans and feeling the curly cabbage.

Betty yelled at me quite often. "You spend too much time

chatting and dawdling," she said. "You should spend more time weeding!"

"Okay! Okay!" I said, wishing the earth would open up and swallow her, so I could be left alone in peace.

Sometimes my friends and I would sneak in the greenhouse and pick a couple of juicy red tomatoes and pluck some mint leaves from their pots. When we chewed on the mint, we pretended it was "Yankee" chewing gum, the kind that children got from American soldiers stationed in England.

At the bottom of the vegetable garden was a fruit orchard where the nuns picked fruit daily and made delicious fruit pies, jams and chutney for all of us to enjoy. When it was a special Holy Holiday, we had clotted cream served with the fruit and pies.

A big chicken coop sat in the back of the greenhouse, and chickens strayed around the garden. Sister Anne, who was in charge of the garden, said, "Girls you must not touch the chickens. It will interfere with them laying eggs."

During the war, food was rationed, and the chickens provided a vital supply of eggs. Each week we had to take supplies to the Red Cross in the village,

"How do chickens lay eggs?" Shirley asked Sister Anne, one day while we were all out working in the garden.

"With the help of the rooster," Sister Anne replied.

"Sister, what does the rooster do to the chicken?" I asked

She said, "Maidy, go and ask the rooster."

I loved to watch the chickens strut around with their free spirits, but I never got close to the rooster.

Finding a pathway, I remembered the little garden it led to, filled with sprays of sweet- smelling flowers bunched together like cauliflowers on each side of the path and hidden by the willow trees that clung together forming an archway.

I stumbled on the large wooden crucifix with the half-naked Christ hanging on it, which stood against a huge white marvel stone. When I was at the orphanage, I knelt in front of this cross many times to pray, hoping that if I pleased God, he would help me to go back home. I would stare and touch the nails that pierced Christ's hands to the cross, Sometimes, I would cry feeling his pain.

Running my fingers around the cross, I thanked God for the many blessings he had bestowed on me.

I sat down on one of the iron benches, which was directly in front of the pond. This was the place where many of the novice nuns came to read their bible and say the rosary. I had walked this path with my friends and my sister many times.

I remember coming here alone when I was eight years old, after I had made my first communion.

I stood looking up at the sky, hidden between the drooping willows while wearing the new rosary Sister Theresa had given to me.

"God, is my Daddy there with you?" I remember calling out. "Please speak to me God."

God did not answer me directly that day, but as I stood there in front of the cross, I heard the sudden rustle of the leaves at a nearby hedgerow, and right in front of me appeared a reddish fat squirrel with eyes that looked like two large coat buttons sitting close together. He had a big bushy tail. In my childish mind the squirrel was Daddy checking up on me. From that day forward the garden became part of Heaven, and the only place I could speak to Daddy.

The squirrels fascinated me. They had become my new family that lived in the willow trees. I loved watching them run up and down the branches, and pull the catkins from the trees. Sometimes I would catch a small catkin and put it in my dress pocket. I placed it under my mattress with my other treasures.

One of my treasures was a sock doll, which I made when I was nine years old, from two socks that I had taken from the dormitory laundry basket. I drew a face with crayons on the front of the sock and stuffed it with the other sock and tied a piece of string around the neck to secure the head.

When Shirley and Ellen saw the doll they squealed out, "Make us a doll like yours, Maidy."

I said, "If you steal the socks, I will make the dolls."

After I made their dolls, we played with them together. My doll was called Tilly. Shirley's doll was named Rose, and Ellen's doll was named Jane.

Villagers donated many toys and games to the orphanage, but they were left in the playroom for everyone to share. The sock dolls belonged to us, and we kept them a secret from the nuns and our other friends. My friends and I played with cut out paper dolls, which we drew on cardboard. We would then draw the clothes on paper for them to wear, but the sock dolls were different. They were soft and we could cuddle them.

A few months later I made a sock dog.

"It looks like a sausage dog," Ellen said.

I named him Sausage Roll.

"Why did you make a dog?" Shirley asked. "You're scared of dogs."

"I don't like big dogs that might bite me," I said.

"Big dogs protect you, and little dogs are scared of strangers," Ellen said.

Sausage Roll became my close friend. I talked to him and my dolly at night in bed and told them all the things that made me happy. My dog wiped my tears away when I was sad, and the only food he needed was cuddles and love.

Shirley, Ellen, and I had been together since nursery school. They were refugees brought from London at age three, and each had lost both parents due to the war. Social Service brought them to Marychurch by train through the Red Cross. They never talked about their parents. We slept in the same dormitory, shared the same books, laughed and played together each day. We went to mass and school and shared tears of sadness and joy. We were like sisters.

Sometimes the three of us would disagree and fight, but we always made up. We had created our own family. On Saturday afternoons we would sit on the red brick wall outside the church and watch the cars pass by us. Sometimes we would talk about the spoiled outdoor girls who went to our school. These students were dropped off at school by fancy cars and some came on the school bus. They wore a school uniform like ours, but it looked different. It was a black gymslip with a white shirt and a black and blue striped tie

Shirley asked, "Why do they look better than us, and we wear the same clothes?"

"Their uniforms are new, and ours is second hand. It never fits quite right," I said.

"I have never worn a blouse that fits me properly," Ellen said.

"You are bigger than I am, and the nuns give you the same size blouse that I wear," Shirley said.

We all laughed and started kicking the gravel around our feet at each other until we saw the priest coming out of the church walking towards us.

"Good morning, Father," we all said in unison.

"You three again!" he said. "What are you doing outside the church?"

"We are waiting for the dining room to open for lunch," I replied.

Father looked down at our shoes and said, "You have been kicking the gravel around the holy grounds."

We looked at each other and chimed in together, "We are sorry, father."

"Tell that to God," he said. "Idle minds are the devil's workshop."

The doors to the dining room opened, and we quickly rushed in, nodding to father as we left.

"Father catches us because he spies on us through his office window," Ellen said.

"Who cares?" I replied. "When I go to confession, I will go to the older priest. I am not telling my sins to anyone but him because I am worried the nuns will find out, and I trust him."

We giggled as girls hurried past us on the way to the dining room. Sometimes we were loud and frivolous and had to be reprimanded by the nuns. They were strict, but very kind to us.

Chapter 5

For What We are about to Receive

I strolled back to the convent, my mind whirling around my childhood days at Marychurch. As I passed the convent window, I could see the retired nuns in the old dining room eating their lunch.

I remember the dining room so well. We lined up for our meals outside the classrooms with our head girl in the front. The younger children went in first, and we marched behind them in silence. It was a large room with long cherry wooden tables and hardwood benches placed in three lines. We all had assigned seats. The nuns served our food on round trays, which were stacked up by the plates on the far side of the room. During the serving, nobody was allowed to walk around the dining room. If you dared to get up, it had to be for a medical reason.

The walls were covered in wallpaper with green art patterns of trees and birds. When I sat down at the table I felt like I was in a forest, especially when the black drapes were drawn.

As I peeked through the window I could see the old furniture was replaced with round maple wood tables and cushioned chairs. The dark drapes had been removed, and sunlight was shining through the windows between the drawn green drapes, making the dining room look larger. I could see fresh paint on the walls, a light beige blending well with the furniture.

As I walked by the dining room, I stopped and took a deep breath. I could still smell the scent of the nun's cooking, the sound of silverware clinking against the bowls, and the soap used to clean everything down once we were done.

I continued to walk towards the rose gardens, and stopped momentarily to sit down at a metal bench that was along the pathway. My mind continued to wander, thinking about dear Sister Catherine Angela walking close to my chair in the dining room. Her long wooden rosary beads brushed up against me as she leaned over to serve a bowl of hot porridge and pour a cup of milk. Sometimes, I refused the milk. I can still hear her voice ringing out, "Maidy, the milk comes from holy cows and it makes the bones strong."

Leaving the table she would say, "Drink up girls, and I mean every drop."

I loved our Sunday dinners but food remained scarce throughout the war and for many years afterward. The nuns produced weekly miracles putting everything together for all of us to eat. The nuns would bake crispy loafs of bread which smelt and tasted so good, especially when it was spread with bright yellow butter and homemade jam.

We said a prayer before each meal to thank God for what we were about to receive. "Bless us Lord for the gifts we are about to receive and make us truly thankful."

You could not touch a morsel of food before we said the prayer. You could not leave the dining room until you finished everything on your plate. A lecture from Mother Superior was certain to come if you waisted food.

She would stare at me and say, "No, not you again Maidy. Do you know food is still on ration and there is not enough food in the shops? Each week the people in the village spend a lot of time queuing for food, and here you are wasting food. Everyone has a ration book including you, and this is what we used to buy meat, cheese, eggs, flour, sugar, and seeds to grow different vegetables."

"I know Mother Superior, but I keep forgetting," I said.

"What is a ration book, Maidy?" she asked.

"The ration book tells you how much food you can buy each week, and it has to last you the whole week." I replied

"Marychurch" holds many fond memories for me even today.

As I left Marychurch and walked along the gray gravel road down Priory Lane, I heard the sound of children laughing. I looked over the stone wall and saw children playing in the backyard. They were kicking a ball around their garden. This was peacetime, and they appeared happy and content.

I walked down to the village, a place that has stood still in time. There were more shops, but the post office with a bright round red post box standing outside the door was in the same place, and the butcher shop was there with different choices of fresh meat sitting in the window. The bakery was also unchanged. We would pass it when we took our Sunday walks with the nuns through the village. In those days, I could only dream about the cream bun that appeared in the bakery after the war.

I was a teenager before I ate a donut or any of the other sweets one sees in English bakeries today.

Across the street was the old sweet shop with tall glass jars of sweets lined up on the wooden shelves, and in the shop window the black licorice and lollipops were standing in a blue china jug. Sweets were also on ration until well after the war. It was a dream for Marychurch children to receive sweets; we had to wait for Christmas to get a candy cane, and this was given to us by the community after we sang Christmas songs to them on the village green during the holidays.

I hated seeing the girls that attended our school during the day go home to their families in the afternoon. The nuns called them "outdoor girls." These girls would come to school pulling out their homemade cakes from their school satchels and would flash them at us, never offering to share.

Jill Evans, an outdoor girl, had red hair and pigtails, and she sat in front of me in class. One day a bag of sweets dropped out of her school bag when she threw the bag under her chair.

We were taking a test that day, so I dropped my pen near her bag and bent down and picked it up with the sweets. Everybody was so engrossed in their test they did not see me in action. I hid the sweets in my knickers. Jill never mentioned she lost the sweets, and later that day I saw her eating from another bag of jelly sweets.

That night when I got into bed with my sock doll and sausage dog I told them what happened at school that day. I pulled the sweets from my knickers and munched on them in the dark. I told my dolly, Tilly, "The girl I took the sweets from is a mean girl."

I hugged my dog. Sausage Roll and I knew that he and Tilly understood.

I made an act of contrition to Jesus and told him that Jill, the ginger haired girl was selfish, as she did not want to share her sweets with anybody, and she is mean.

That night I prayed for a long time and begged Jesus to forgive me. I knew I had broken the sixth commandment. Thou shall not steal.

I felt unworthy of His love. I banged my head up and down against the wall for my punishment. I finished the sweets that night. I did not want to share them with anyone, not even my friends.

Our dormitory was a large room with long beams covering the ceiling. The interior of the room was paneled with dark colored wood and the windows were covered with black blinds which were drawn most of the time. There were ten beds on each side of the room. My bed was located on the end facing a wooden ramshackle hut, which the nuns called a shanty. This was the place where Sister Teresa slept. The room had black cotton curtains hung over the window, which were put there during the war.

Sister Teresa said, "We use these curtains to prevent the German planes from seeing us. The village is entirely blacked out with no lights after sundown. It is dangerous to be outside during the blackout because there are no street lights, and cars drive around without lights on."

"Sister," I asked. "Who checks to see that people were safe outside?"

"The village wardens," she said. "They are like policemen and they walk up and down the street checking that no light can be seen outside. If they see even a small light from a torch inside the house, they shout, 'Put out the lights!' After the war was over, many homes continued to keep their black curtains hanging up, including Marychurch," Sister Teresa said.

"Why do we still have the curtains hanging in the dormitory?" Ellen asked.

"In the winter they keep the dormitory more insulated, and in the summer they block our day light to enable you to sleep," Sister replied.

My bed was located in the corner of the room up against the wall. When I stood up on my toes at the top of the bed, I could slide my head under the black curtains and look out the window and see the back entrance to the church. I was the watchdog for our dormitory and alerted the girls when the nuns were leaving church and would come to the dormitory.

Long wooden beams ran across the ceiling, and other beams reached down to the floor near our beds and in the center of the room. At night when the nuns were at Vespers, their night prayers, we would climb up on the beams and swing on them like monkeys. I had so much fun hanging on those beams upside down. But one evening my friend Shirley fell off one of the beams and twisted her ankle.

When Sister Teresa saw her limping at morning mass she said, "Shirley, why are you limping?"

Shirley did not tell her she fell off the beam. She said, "I was running in the dormitory and twisted my ankle."

Sister glanced at Ellen and I, knowing we were all friends, said, "What happened to Shirley?"

"She fell when she was running," I said.

If we had told sister the truth she would have spanked her for climbing up on the beams. The other girls in the dorm stuck by us and said, "Shirley fell when she was running, Sister."

Sister Teresa looked at Shirley and said, "Shirley, go to the nurse's office and have her check your ankle."

Sister turned her face towards us and the look on her face told me she did not believe us, but she never mentioned the incident again.

When Sister Teresa came into her shanty room at night, everyone was in bed with the lights out. I could often hear soft mellow music coming through her door. I had listened to radio music, but this music was different. Notes came from a piano that gripped on to your heart. I loved the sound as it soothed my soul before I fell asleep.

I was lying awake coughing one night, and Sister came out of her room to check on me and give me some nasty tasting cough syrup. I asked her about the music. She said, "This is God's music created by three famous composers, Mozart, Beethoven, and Chopin. It is music that God has provided us to rest our brain."

"Sister, it sounds beautiful," I said through my coughs.

"Check their autobiographies in the school library, Maidy," she said. "If you need help, ask God, and he will help you find their autobiographies."

"How do I speak to God?" I asked.

"Maidy, you speak to God with silence around you, and in silence God will speak to you," she said. "He is there for your needs Maidy."

"Thank you, Sister Teresa. Good night."

"Good night, Maidy."

I laid back on my pillow staring at the beams hanging from the ceiling, and thought about God. What does He look like, and why can't people see Him? I know what an angel looks like. God has been around forever, but who made God?

"Goodnight, God," I said. I know full well you exist, but only through the Holy Spirit you placed in my soul because I believe in you, God.

Chapter 6

A World of Knowledge, Comfort and Peace

When you walked into the school library, there was a musty smell of old books, providing one with a sense of mystery and awe. In the center was an old maple wooden table, surrounded with hardback chairs. Two worn chocolate brown leather armchairs stood by long narrow windows facing the garden. This was my favorite place to sit and watch the birds chirping in the fruit trees.

Dusty shelves of books were lined against each wall in the library. If you were to reach up and pull one from the bookshelf, it would have a thick cover and was quite heavy for me to hold as a child. I loved turning the pages of the book slowly as they were quite sturdy and some books had pictures with light tissue paper in between. You had to be careful with the tissue paper as it crinkled and could easily tear.

When I curled up in the chair, I pressed my nose against the leather, as I loved the special smell that lingered in my nostrils. A huge red brick fireplace, which burnt black lumps of coal, was lit up during the cold winter nights giving a warm feeling around the room.

When I was ten years old, I could stay up a little later before going to bed. I felt special as Mother Superior would read from a classic book to us. Sometimes she would ask me to read as I was a good reader. I can remember listening to Sister Mary's soft voice reading *Jane Eyre, Little Women* and *Pride and Prejudice.* I would walk right into the story book and join the characters as they had become my new friends.

At night when I crept into bed I would talk to the mother from *Little Women* and pretend she was mine. I asked her to hold me tight and adopt me. I could feel her tenderness and listened to her soft-spoken voice telling me I could be her other daughter. Her kindness wrapped around me, giving me the love for which I hungered.

I fell in love with Mr. Rochester from *Jane Eyre* and cried when Jane and Mr. Rochester broke his relationship off on their wedding day, after Jane learned Mr. Rochester's secret. I cried even harder when Jane returned to find a broken and lost Mr. Rochester after his home was in ruins. I was relieved when at the end of Jane's visit she decided to stay and take care of him, and they started a family together.

When I think of my childhood at Marychurch, my most cherished memory is spending time in the library. I remember the rustling sound of the nun's rosary brushing up against a wooden cart, and seeing a novice nun rolling the trolley into the library before bed time, to serve us a mug of steaming hot cocoa and rich tea biscuits. Books became my family and the library had become as important as the church for my development and growth.

On Saturday evenings, my friends and I would go to the library and pick up a pair of socks and a wooden toadstool from a wicker to darn the socks of children living at Marychurch. The socks had holes in the heels and toes, and the nuns taught us how to darn them by making ladders over the holes with the yarn and weaving the yarn in and out of the ladders as you would weave a basket.

The wooden toadstool was shaped like a mushroom with

a short handle. I placed it inside the sock for support to enable me to darn the hole by holding the wooden handle.

I can still hear Sister Catherine's words: "Girls, the darning has to be smooth, not lumpy or you will have to rip it out and redo it." It took me a few pairs of socks before I did a good job. The nuns also taught me how to knit and sew small items.

When I was eleven years old, I entered a knit-a-square competition. I had to knit a square the same size as a washcloth and use my imagination for a pattern. I knitted an airplane on my square.

I showed it to Sister Teresa, and she said, "Maidy, I am so proud of you!"

I won first prize and received a book by Enid Blyton, a famous children's author. The book's title was *Five Run Away Together*. The story was about five children who ran away from home and how they survived during the war.

I enjoyed this book so much that when I found out it came in a sequel, I had to go to the village library, which was one mile from Marychurch, to check the books out to read. If I went to the public library, it had to be with a senior girl.

My sister Jeanette was a senior, and when I bumped into her that night after benediction she said, "Shirley told me you were looking for me."

"Jeanette, you know the Enid Blyton books?" I said. "I want to read more of her books, but I have to check them out in the public library."

She answered, "I go there each week to check out books, and they have many Enid Blyton books. She is not a classic writer, though. Won't the sisters object to you reading her?"

"I like her writing, and I want you to ask Mother Superior's permission to take me to the library," I said.

"I take piano lessons from Mother Superior, and she said I was her best student," Jeanette said. "I think she likes me. I don't think she'll object to you coming with me to the library."

"Great!" I said.

I already knew Jeanette was one of Mother Superior's favorite students, since she chose Jeanette to play a couple hymns for the children's morning mass, which was held once a month. Whenever I needed to find Jeanette, I could find her in the music room practicing on the piano or reading her library book. She had few friends who were smart students like her, and my sister never got into trouble with the nuns like I did.

The downside for me was the teachers who had Jeanette in their class expected that same good behavior from me. They were sadly disappointed. I was smart and did well in my school studies, but the nuns always said I asked too many questions, especially about religion. The nuns felt I shouldn't question words spoken from the Bible, since these were the literal words of God.

Who was I to ask how the Virgin Mary got pregnant?

How does Jesus' blood turn into wine?

Who made God?

Why can't I see Jesus?

Whenever I asked a question, I was told to sit down and stay quiet or I would get smacked on my knuckles with the ruler for daring to ask such questions. The next day I saw my sister at breakfast. She greeted me.

"Maidy, I got permission to take you to the library."

I had a big grin on my face and thanked her.

"You must be happy," Shirley said. "I don't like books like you do, but it is a good way to leave Marychurch for a couple of hours."

I looked straight at Shirley and Ellen, who were standing in front of me, wanting to know if Jan would take them with me to the library, and I said, "No, my sister will not take the three of us. She already told me you would ask me and said she was not going to take that responsibility."

Ellen replied, "I don't want to go to a place with hundreds of books. I have enough with my school books."

My sister and I were very excited to spend some time

together. The following week we walked to the library, passing the fish and chip shop, the smell of battered fish leaving us feeling hungry. We walked slowly by the produce market lined with fruit stands outside of the shop. Apples, peaches, cherries, and plums filled the wooden crates and always looked ripe for eating. As we walked by the apples I knocked two out of their wooden crate, they started rolling down the cobbled street. I picked up the apples that had landed in the drain, and started to run with them. Jeanette followed close behind me.

"Maidy, What do you think you are doing?" Jeanette yelled. "I saw you knocking the apples out of the box. We cannot do this again or else we will lose our privileges going to the library."

"Okay," I said, pausing to catch my breath. "The fruit belongs to God because he told Adam and Eve to eat from the fruit trees in the Garden of Eden."

"Yes, I know," my sister said, "but don't forget they ate the apple from the tree that God had forbidden them to touch, and now we all have to die because of them."

"Jeanette, what happens when we die?" I asked.

"We will live in a place called Heaven with God and the angels where there will be no pain and we will never die again," she said.

"It will be boring there," I said. "You don't need food up in Heaven,

and I want to eat chocolate biscuits, and cream buns each day."

"Maidy, you need not worry about Heaven because you have a long time before you die," Jeanette said. "I will come and get you, because I will die before you."

"I want to die with you," I said. "We can go to Heaven together and see our Daddy."

We both sat down on the iron bench for a rest and bit into our apples. We were close to the music shop and could see a beautiful piano sitting in the shop window. My sister loved playing the piano.

"One day I will play beautiful music and own a piano like this one," she said.

"I will sit in your living room and read my books while you play," I said.

After finishing our apples, we got up from the bench and continued to make our way to the library. As we walked down the stone path, we caught sight of the library from behind two mulberry trees. It was a red brick building with stone steps leading up to the entrance.

We climbed the front steps and went inside to the front desk, where I met Mrs. Finkle, the Librarian. She was tall and thin with boney features and wore her hair up in a tight bun. Brown rim glasses were perched on her nose. She had two beady eyes peeping out at me. She asked me to fill out a form with my personal information.

Frowning at me, she said, "I will give you a library card to check books out of the library. It permits you to check out two books, and they are to be returned on the stamped date."

"Yes, Mrs. Finkle," I said.

She looked at my sister and said, "Tell your sister the library rules. Be sure to let her know what happens to children who misbehave. Especially children from Marychurch."

She took a deep breath and looked directly at me and said, "Any problems whatsoever will be reported to Mother Superior and your library card will be revoked."

"Yes, Mrs. Finkle, I understand," I said.

I was proud of my library card and felt grown up when Mrs. Finkle gave it to me. I stood there and glanced at my card. I looked up and my eyes wandered around the library, looking at all the shelves full of books waiting to be read.

"This is the best present in the world," I said.

She smiled, and showed me the children's section where there were many choices of books I wanted to read. I stood there in awe, staring at the books grouped by authors. I could come here every day and would never be able to go through all these books.

I turned around and could not believe my eyes when I saw two full shelves of Enid Blyton books. She wrote about everything, from the circus, to the farm animals, magic, boarding schools, and two series of adventure books. I picked the second and third book of the series of *Five Children Go on an Adventure* and *Five Run Off to the Circus*.

I met Jeanette at the checkout desk. Mrs. Finkle was standing behind the desk and said, "Do you know how to turn book pages, so they will not be damaged?"

"Yes, I will use a bookmark," I said.

As we were leaving I said to Jeanette, "I would not want to upset Mrs. Finkle."

Jeanette and I went to the library once a week. Mrs. Finkle seemed anxious when she saw girls from Marychurch enter the library and would constantly keep her eyes on us.

One day as I was returning two books to the library, Mrs. Finkle took my sister aside, and whispered in her ear, "I don't think Maidy reads the books she checks out. She returns them too soon to the library."

As I checked my books in, Mrs. Finkle said, "Maidy, have you read the books from beginning to end?"

"Yes," I said. "I know the story from beginning to the end, and I am a fast reader."

"Maidy, let's see what you can remember," Mrs. Finkle said. She carefully thumbed through pages, stopping periodically to ask me questions. When I answered them to her satisfaction. She finally said, "I guess you are a fast reader."

When my sister and I walked to the library, we would pass many buildings that had been demolished by Germans bombs. They were tagged with big signs saying, "Danger! Stay away from these buildings." This included houses, shops, schools and the Anglican Christian church, which was a block from Marychurch..

Mother Superior told us in the school library while we were darning socks that we had many blessings bestowed on us during the war.

She said, "Not too long ago, during the day, a German plane hit the cross on the steeple of our church with its wings and jettisoned its bomb, which shot over to the Anglican Christian church a few hundred yards away."

Children were in the classroom attending Sunday school and twenty one children and several teachers were killed. They were laid to rest in their church yard.

Sister said, "Marychurch had a long mass served for the children and the people from the village. The nuns from Marychurch were sad and shaken for weeks because of their deaths."

One day after Jeanette and I came home from the public library, she took me to visit the cemetery at the back of the Anglican church where we found the children's graves, each bearing a cross. We sat on the ground and prayed for the children's souls. I was too young to understand the war.

My sister said, "Air raid-sirens made a terrible wailing noise when the German planes came to drop bombs. You had to go to the shelter quickly. Maidy, the nuns carried you to the bomb shelter in a siren suit made from a blanket by the nuns. The suit kept you warm in the cold shelter. I was scared of the air-raids and hated the rubber gas masks. The rubber mask smelled and made me feel sick, especially as I had to carry it with me most of the time."

"Why did you need rubber gas masks?" I asked.

She said, "We were all given rubber gas masks in case poison gas dropped from the German planes. It was all so scary, but the planes frightened me most of all. I still hear that noise in my sleep"

"I hate the Germans!" I said. "They killed our Daddy."

"Whenever an air raid started, the nuns would run and carry the babies to the shelter, and as soon as I arrived I would look for you," she said. "After I saw you, I was happy, and the nuns would let me sit with you," she said with a deep sigh.

Many times on our way home from the library we would stop by one of the bomb sites and dig among the rubble with old metal knitting needles that we had found in the rubbish bin behind the secondhand shop in the village.

Jeanette kept them in her school satchel to use to look for treasures at the bombsites. We discovered old jewelry, pieces of shrapnel, old tins and books and pots and pans. This collection was very precious to us. We found an old rusty biscuit tin and put our found treasures inside and pressed the lid shut.

We buried the tin under the chestnut tree in the church graveyard where the children's graves were located, creating a secret. We left the tin to share with them as they were our new friends and added more stuff whenever we went to the bomb site.

One rainy day after returning from the library we went to check on the biscuit tin and found it was gone. We searched high and low, but it was nowhere to be found.

I cried and told Jeanette, "The dead children stole our biscuit tin."

I went around the graves asking each grave, "Did you take the biscuit tin?"

My sister yelled, "I hope they have taken it, and they are happy with these special gifts from us."

Sometimes during our walk to the library Jeanette would say, "Do you think Mum is ever going to take us home?"

I would kick the gravel on the road as I hated talking about Mum. I didn't know who she was, but Jeanette said, "She is beautiful, like a movie star."

"I don't care if I see her again, but I want to see Daddy," I said.

"Maidy, Daddy is in Heaven and you will see him when you die."

"How do you know he is in Heaven?' I asked.

She replied, "Because he is watching over us like an angel."

"Why do we have to talk about Mum and Dad?" I asked. "I always get upset when you bring up Mum."

My sister replied, "I'm sorry Maidy. I won't mention them anymore."

I became silent and my thoughts were on Daddy. I worried about him and hoped he was happy in Heaven, but what did he do all day? Could he see me?

I went to a nearby fence and started to bang my head up and down until I heard Jeanette say, "Stop it, Maidy! Stop it!"

I felt better after banging my head. This was a habit I had whenever I felt angry or guilty. It was a way for me to control myself. It prevented me from lashing out at others. Sometimes I felt like I was going crazy as there were so many questions rattling in my head regarding my parents that I did not know how to answer.

I often wondered why so many children at Marychurch went home to their parents after the war. I had a mother. Why didn't I go home as well?

Jeanette and I arrived back at Marychurch and she said, "I will see you later, Maidy."

I turned the other way and ran towards my friends who were going to the dining room for tea. I loved teatime as we ate jam and cucumber sandwiches and had pots of weak tea poured into our cups by the nuns. I loved the sponge cake as it looked like a big round bun with cream and jam in the middle. The nuns would cut the cake so we all got an equal serving. They wore brown cord belts wrapped around their waist which dangled down near our chairs as they leaned forward cutting the cake.

When we spoke to each other it was almost a whisper. If we

shouted too loudly, the nun would come over to our table to tell us there was to be complete silence until the end of the meal.

We shouted a few times at our table, especially when we discussed books we had read. We argued about the characters of the book, especially the leading male character. This was followed by deciding together who he should marry if we were a character in the book and how many babies we would have. As a group, we started laughing out loud, attracting attention from other students in the dining room and the Sister in charge.

"I could see me with Mr. Rochester," I said, "walking in the garden, holding his hand and him stooping down to pick some flowers and him kissing me."

"Oh no! Not Mr. Rochester," said Shirley in a loud voice. "He is mean to Jane, and he had the nerve to marry her, when he already had a wife."

Before anyone else said something, I yelled out, "I love Mr. Rochester."

Suddenly, there was silence in the dining room and Sister Teresa came over and said, "You girls will not speak one word until you leave the dining room."

After the meal we walked out to the playground and started laughing.

After the event in the dining room, my friends gave me the nickname, "Jane Eyre."

Chapter 7

Nature Walks with Sister Margaret

I stood by the iron railing on Priory Road thinking of my childhood. I was seeing the many changes that had occurred at the place I once called home. I took a long, hard, long look at Marychurch. There was no more orphanage and school, but there was still the beautiful old church standing majestic with dark clouds hovering in the background. I walked over to the gardens where I had watched the red sunset dissolving into the night of darkness many times before from my dormitory window.

I loved walking by the rows of vegetables with joyful memories while smelling fresh lilac from the bushes scattered along the walkway. I thought of dear Sister Margaret who was in charge of the garden and taught us nature study.

My school friends and I enjoyed the Thursday morning nature walks with Sister. She opened our eyes to all God's creations through nature. I walked alongside her and stopped to smell fresh dug earth with shafts of light striking through the trees.

Sister said, "A strong wind blowing from the trees is compassion from God to strengthen us."

Sister Margaret was stocky in build and a strict teacher but very fair in judgment. Her sprigs of gray hair stuck out around her moon shaped face under her black veil. She spoke in a gentle voice unless she got agitated, and then her voice changed and became louder and very matter of fact on the point she was trying to get across to you. She was one of my favorite nuns. She had an air about her which demanded respect. You always knew where you stood with her. Especially when she made a statement and gave constructive criticism, you listened and learned.

Sister Margaret would take us on the downs where there was a walking path close to the red clay cliffs overlooking the sea. On the other side was country and farm buildings.

I loved our walks in the springtime. During our walk Sister would suddenly say, "Girls stand still. Take a deep breath, and close your eyes. Listen to the Holy Spirit, through the sound of the ocean. Do you hear the rustle of leaves, and the whistle of the wind through the trees?"

She would tell us to open our eyes and look at God's creation all around us; the gray blue sky, the sheep, and cows who were grazing in the nearby meadows close to a babbling brook.

There was something magical in the air when she spoke in her soft voice. You felt that the sky would open up, and you would get that first glimpse of heaven. When Sister pointed out the different flowers, which grew in clusters along the side of our paths, she described them as new life entering the world through God's hands.

"Girls, look at the white crocuses and yellow daffodils peeping through the grass, and look at the blackberry and gooseberry bushes, which have sprouted their small berries and will soon be ripe enough to pick. This is God's creation."

My friends and I loved looking at the yellow carpet of buttercups and white daisies in the fields. When the weather got warmer, we would take off our shoes and socks and squish our feet in the grass. I could feel the cool grass poking through my toes. It made me want to giggle and jump in the air.

I remember sitting on the soft velvet green grass with my friends and making long daisy chains, which were worn around our necks. The fun time was picking a buttercup and placing it under each other's chin to see if your neck showed a yellow light. If it did, your guardian angel was close to you.

When the flowers and fruit were budding in spring, Sister Margaret said, "Girls you cannot pick the flowers or fruit until they are in full bloom."

"Sister, what happens to the flowers when the strong sea breezes come up from the ocean?" I asked.

She said, "The flowers will tremble like we do when we suddenly get cold. Mother earth will protect nature from the winds, and the foam from the ocean waves will refresh them."

When we went on our nature study walks, Sister brought some gooseberry, plum, or strawberry jam sandwiches for our lunch. We would sit down in a field of clover under a big spreading chestnut tree and eat them. I loved licking the oozing jam popping out of the bread. We had to say a prayer before eating the sandwiches.

"I don't know why we have to pray all the time, Shirley complained. "Maidy, did you see those kids passing by with their parents laughing at us?"

Ellen, who had thoughts of becoming a nun, scowled at Shirley and said, "Mother Superior believes prayers are the food for your soul, and if you want to starve your soul, don't pray."

Shirley looked at me, "Which one of us is correct, Maidy?" She asked.

Ignoring Shirley, I looked at my friends and said, "Sister is getting ready to continue our walk."

Each time we went on walks we did a study of every part of nature from the curling waves and changing tides from the ocean, to the misty early fog. We studied the trees, the meadows, and the cows and sheep that graze the grass, and all the creeks and ponds that we would pass by.

I remember spending one afternoon at an old dusty water mill where my friends and I picked up frogs and petted them.

They were slimy and dark green, but I loved to hear the croaky sound that came from within them. I was amazed to think these frogs came from the tiny tadpoles that I had watched swimming in the pond.

I will never forget the day when Shirley kept a frog to bring back to Marychurch.

"I will wrap him up with my handkerchief and keep it in my pocket," she exclaimed.

I said, "What are you going to wipe your nose with? We are given one handkerchief a week."

She laughed, "I will share yours and Ellen's."

"What are you going to feed it?" Ellen asked.

"They eat anything," Shirley answered

I replied, "They don't eat human food."

At that moment Sister came and stood in front of us and said, "You girls are up to something. You have been dawdling around the pond long enough."

Ellen answered, "We were talking about the frogs and were wondering what they eat?"

"Frogs have long sticky tongues and eat insects, snails, worms, slugs, mice and fish, Sister said. "They drink water by sucking it into their body while they are swimming, and when they are on land, water is absorbed through their skin."

Suddenly Ellen said, "Oh no!"

The frog that Shirley had in her pocket jumped out on the grass in front of Sister Margaret's feet.

Sister looked directly at Shirley and said, "Pick the frog up and put him in the pond where he belongs. You are not taking him back to Marychurch!"

She then looked at Ellen and me and said, "Empty out your pockets."

We both emptied our pockets with leaves and rocks we had picked up during our walk.

Sister then gathered us together in a group and said, "Girls, do not pick up frogs or insects as they are God's creatures and belong on the land and in the ocean."

We answered, "Yes, Sister Margaret."

"Today we will study the weeping willow tree," Sister said. "I want each one of you to pick a catkin from the tree and we will discuss it and for your homework you will do more research and write two paragraphs on what we discussed about the tree."

We all sat down on the grass as she continued talking. "You need not write these notes down," Sister said. "If you listen, you might learn something. The weeping willow's beauty comes from its sweeping low branches that droop to create a 'falling canopy.' This tree is one of the fastest growing shade trees, growing up from six to eight feet each year. They start out thin, with only a few branches that point upwards against the trunk. After reaching a height of ten feet. They spread out more branches which arch out to form the weeping canopy. They are very adaptable to all kinds of soils and growing conditions and these trees even help prevent soil erosion."

Sister stopped talking and said, "Everybody stand up. Girls, you can add into your homework what we discussed today, but from each of you I need some fresh information."

We all answered, "Yes, Sister Margaret."

As we started our walk back to Marychurch, I saw a woman pushing a pram with two young children in it, and a boy was walking beside her holding her hand. She stopped as we passed by. I took a quick look at her and she met my eyes with a smile. I started wondering what made my mother stay away from her girls for ten years.

How can you not want to take care of a baby you have brought into this world? How could you live with yourself knowing you have children somewhere, and not feel the guilt of rejection? I will never ever forgive her for leaving Jeanette and me, especially after our father had been taken from us.

I looked at Shirley and said, "If God blesses me with

children, I will never leave them no matter what obstacles crossed my path."

Shirley replied, "It is worse for you Maidy, as my Mum died in the London Blitz, but your Mum ran away from you and Jeanette."

I did not like to hear what Shirley said, so I walked ahead of her.

Suddenly Sister Margaret was walking beside me and said, "Maidy, you are in deep thoughts. You did not hear me call your name?"

"I am thinking bad things about my mother," I said.

"What things?" Sister asked.

"How can I ever forgive her for what she did to my sister and me?" I said. "She deserted us, and I hate her!"

In her gentle voice, Sister said, "Try not to fill your heart with hate, Maidy, as you will be the one to carry the burden of pain for the rest of your life. You must give it time and know that God is watching over you and will be there when you stumble. Hold out your hand and God will catch you when you fall."

We reached the gates of Marychurch and I said, "Thank you Sister Margaret."

She answered, "God be with you always."

Chapter 8

A Thousand Streams Run through My Mind

Whenever I think of Marychurch, my mind becomes a thousand streams of memories. One stream flows towards me taking me back to my childhood and my outside trips from Marychurch with my sister. These trips increased after the war, which made us happy.

Because we were older, Jeanette was twelve years and I was eight-and-a-half, Daddy's two old aunts, Aunt Susanna and Aunt Lucretia started visiting us twice a month. We also began to see more of my mother. Then we began to visit all of them in their homes. Every other Sunday we went on the double decker bus to visit my mother in Newton Abbot. And every other weekend we spent at our aunts' cottage.

When the aunts came to Marychurch, they fetched us on Friday morning and brought us back Sunday afternoon. My grandmother had died giving birth to my father, and my grandfather, their brother, raised him. My father was seven-years-old when my grandfather died, and my aunts raised him to manhood.

I found out from my aunts why we had not seen Mum during wartime. We overheard them discussing her in their kitchen. Jeannette and I were supposed to be sleeping in the small bedroom at the back of their cottage, but we were wide-awake listening to these old ladies talk about our mother.

Aunt Susanna told Aunt Lucretia, "It's disgusting that Babs had got married so soon after Juan's death and never mentioned to her new husband that she had two daughters tucked away at Marychurch."

Aunt Susanna replied, "Babs should be ashamed of herself and get down on her knees and pray to the Lord to forgive her for her evil ways. Thank the lord that Juan had not known this side of her character."

Jeanette and I lay in our bed and had to cover our mouths with our blankets as we were giggling, knowing our aunts were strict Christian Scientists.

It pleased me that they disliked my mother. They could see how selfish she was. Now I know why she didn't come and visit us.

I remember one Sunday afternoon Mother Superior requesting Jeanette and I to come to her office. I was nine-and-a-half and Jeanette was thirteen. As we walked into the office, a big surprise was waiting for us. A beautiful tall slim lady with long black hair was sitting on a chair opposite Mother Superior.

Jeanette knew who she was, but I did not recognize her. My sister turned to the lady and said, "Hello, Mummy".

She stood up, and I stared at this beautiful lady who was wearing a navy blue suit and a white silk blouse tucked underneath. She had been crying as her face looked swollen from her tears. She came towards us but I hid behind Jeanette.

Mother Superior said, "Your Mother has moved closer to the convent, and you girls will be going to visit her in Newton Abbot, where she lives, every other Sunday. You will catch a bus that will take you directly to Newton Abbot from Marychurch village and your mother will meet you at the bus station, and you will return to Marychurch the same day."

"Do we go after Mass or after breakfast, Sister?" Jeanette asked.

Mother Superior said, "You will attend Mass and then go directly after you have had your breakfast. On Sundays the bus leaves every hour from the village to Newton Abbot."

Mum sat back down on her chair and said, "I have brought you girls some pretty clothes to wear when you come and visit me, so you need not wear your school clothes."

I looked at the open box of clothes and saw colors of brown, green, and two knitted hats the same color red.

I looked at her and said, "How do you know they will fit us? You don't know our size."

"I contacted Mother Superior for both your clothes sizes." She replied.

I looked down on the floor and wished it would open up as I could not believe how words came out of her mouth with such calmness, almost as if she visited us every week.

Mother Superior interrupted my thoughts and said to my mother, "You should get acquainted with the girls today. I will leave you together for one hour."

When the door closed, I can remember a long silence. Jeanette and I stood there dumbfounded, and then Mum said, "Girls I am so happy to see you."

Jeanette broke down and cried, "Mummy, are we ever going to go home?"

"As soon as I can find a house big enough for our family, you will come home," she said.

"You mean you have been looking for a house we can live in all these years?" I said. "Well, I want to stay at Marychurch, and I don't want to live with you."

Jeanette said, "I want to go home."

"Maidy, I know you're upset, but I love you and want you to be with me as soon as possible," Mum said.

I looked at her through tears of anger and said, "What do

you know about love? Where were you all these years? Looking for a house!"

Mum stood up directly from her chair and said, "Girls, when your father was killed I could not take care of you or your brother. His pension was not enough for us to live on, and I had to go back to nursing and work."

I yelled at her, "Who throws a baby in an orphanage?"

Mum sat down and cried. "Please don't get upset. The nuns have taken good care of you, and I promise you I will bring you home as soon as possible."

I yelled out, "Who are you? I don't know you. Marychurch is my home."

She sat on the leather chair with a big white handkerchief wiping her eyes.

Jeanette yelled, "Stop it, Maidy! Stop it!'

I looked at her and said, "You don't mind that she left you all these years in an orphanage? We might as well be nuns as they raised us."

"Yes, I mind, but Mummy is here now and I want to go home." she replied

Mum changed the subject with a strained voice, and said, "You have a young half-sister, Barbara, and your brother Chris is at home with me. You also have a new Daddy."

To hear what Mum said was like a lid coming off a steaming kettle. I was boiling!

"I don't want a new Daddy. I have one in Heaven, and I don't need another sister. I have Jeanette." I screamed out at the top of my voice.

Mum stood up and said, "I am sorry girls. I wish your father had not got killed and things would have been different for us all, but he was taken from us and would have wanted you with the nuns while I worked."

I looked at Jeanette with surprise when she belted out, "No, Daddy would never have wanted us in an orphanage. It was you Mummy, and Aunt Ruby."

I looked at Mum's shocked face after what Jeanette said to her.

"When did my brother come home?" I asked

Mum said, "He was at St. Vincent. It closed after the war ended, and I brought him home."

Jeanette said, "We had wondered where our brother was, and we never talked about him, as we thought he was dead."

"No, no, he is fine and is looking forward to seeing you both."

She stretched her arms out and tried to reach both of us and said, "When we get to know each other everything will be fine, and when I find a house, you can come home."

"This is my home," I said.

Jeanette ignored me and said, "How long will it take for you to find a house?"

"I am on the list for a Council house and when I get a call from them, I will come and get you both after we move in." she replied

"What is a council house?" I asked.

"Because your Daddy got killed in the war it entitles us to live in a lower income home," Mum said.

Mother Superior came back into the room and my mother left after saying goodbye to us both. Jeanette and I were crying.

Mother Superior looked at us with her kind face, and said, "I will pray for you both and hope you will find a place in your hearts to forgive your mother for the long absence."

We looked at her teary eyed and I said, "Are you going to take care of our new clothes?"

"Yes," she said, "but when you visit your mother, you will wear these clothes."

We left the office and walked outside to the front of the church. I turned to my sister and said, "I hate Mummy."

"We have to give her a chance, Maidy."

That night I tossed and turned and banged my head against the wall. I wondered what really happened to my father. I knew from Sister Teresa that the Germans killed him, but what if they were wrong and he was looking for us? The next morning after mass I told Shirley and Ellen I needed to walk alone in the garden, and I would skip breakfast.

They both looked at me and said, "We understand you are hurting, but we are here for you when you need us."

I continued my own walking down the garden path and stopped near the willow tree to listen to the birds chirping and watch the squirrels whispering within the branches of the tree. I paused by the cross and said, "God, I cannot forgive my mother deserting my sister and me especially after losing our daddy. I am mad at Daddy for getting killed."

I banged my head against the cross and suddenly I heard a gentle voice. It was Sister Teresa.

She said, "Maidy, I am sorry for the pain you are going through but it is not your fault. Mother Superior told me that your mother came to see you yesterday. When you did not come into the dining room for breakfast, I knew you would be here with God."

I looked at her with teary eyes and bit my lower lip.

"Sometimes we don't understand why things happen that cause us pain," she said, "but God loves you and he will listen to your prayers."

"Sister, he took both my parents from me," I said.

"Maidy, God didn't take your parents from you. The enemy killed your father in the war, and your mother chose the path she took."

"I hate my mother, and I never want to see her again."

Sister bent down in front of me and said, "Maidy, God is forgiving and you must learn to forgive her and turn the hate into love."

Sister Teresa put her arms around me and hugged me.

I said, "I feel sad and sick to my stomach, but I will pray to God to help me to be happy again."

She smiled and said. "God will listen, because you are special, and he loves you very much."

She left me standing by the cross, and I leaned against it asking God for help and forgiveness. I watched the squirrels running up and down the trees and wished I could be as happy as they were.

I walked towards the school, and my two friends Shirley and Ellen were coming towards me. We hugged each other. They knew how sad I was and together we said,

"Friends need friends, and we are friends forever."

Shirley and Ellen lost both of their parents in the London Blitz. When the Germans bombed the city of London thirty-six times in one day, Shirley and Ellen became orphans. They were brought to Marychurch by train. We became friends in the first grade. In 1946 both were put up for adoption, after waiting a year after the war in case a family member might turn up to claim them.

They had seen many prospective families but nobody adopted them. Prospective parents were looking for younger children.

"No one will adopt me because I have crossed eyes," Shirley said.

"That's not true," I said.

"Yes it is true," she said. "A family was looking for an older child and when they saw me, they wanted to know what was wrong with my eyes and walked away from me."

Ellen said, "You don't want to go with mean parents who judge you by your eyes. I don't want to be adopted as I told Mother Superior I want to become a novice nun."

"I don't want to go and live with my mother," I said.

"I don't want to say goodbye to you," answered Ellen.

Shirley said, "Okay. We all stay together until we graduate from school."

Ellen chimed in and said, "We can all be novice nuns."

I answered, "I want to get married one day and have kids, and I will never treat them like my parents."

Shirley said, "Why did your mother take so long to see you?"

Ellen said, "Maybe she wants Maidy because she is no longer a baby and can help her with the housework."

"Sister told me that during the war children could leave school at fourteen years and they could work in housekeeping or other labor jobs," I said.

"I know Maidy, but Sister said when the war ended the government changed the rule to fifteen to leave school," Ellen replied.

Shirley said, "You and Jeanette will be like the ugly sisters in Cinderella."

I yelled out loud: "I hate Mum. What I don't understand is how my sister can be so nice to her."

"Your sister acts differently because she keeps her feelings inside, and you tell people the way you feel, and that's what we love about you Maidy," Ellen replied.

Shirley said, "I agree with Ellen, but I know your sister is hurting inside and she is older than you. She is a senior and will be graduating from school soon. Time is going by too fast for her."

"I wish I was the older sister and had graduated from Marychurch," I said. "I don't want to go to another school without you. Why did my mother have to come here and ruin our lives again? I hate her."

With tears streaming down my eyes I looked at both of my friends and they were both crying. We looked at each other and started to laugh at Ellen making funny faces at us.

"Come on you two," Ellen said. "We should play hopscotch to cheer us up."

Playing hopscotch in the churchyard was how we met in the first grade and became friends.

I remember that day like it was yesterday. It was our midday break, and we were standing waiting to play hopscotch and a mean girl named Gillian jumped ahead of Shirley, who yelled it was her turn to play. Gillian pushed Shirley to the ground and called her cross-eyed and kicked her. Ellen and I came to her defense by pushing Gillian and grabbing her hair. Sister Anne, who was monitoring the playground, came over to see what the commotion was all about, and sent all four of us to Mother Superior for punishment.

Mother Superior stood up as we walked into her office. After hearing what happened from Sister Anne, she whacked us on the hands with a wooden ruler, and confined us to the classroom during the breaks for the next two days to write, "I will not hit or push another girl in my school so help me God" one hundred times. It was during that time Shirley, Ellen and I united and became the best of friends, and Gillian never bothered us again. When I go back to my memories of Marychurch I am so gratified for the friendship of Shirley and Ellen. These girls supported me during my childhood and taught me the true meaning of friendship.

Chapter 9

Visiting Mum

It had been two weeks since my mother's visit to Marychurch, and today was Saturday. I was coming out of the church after the Benediction service with Shirley and Ellen, and my sister Jeanette was waiting for me by the church door.

"Maidy, tomorrow is Sunday and we will see Mum," she said.

I looked at her and said, "You go. I don't want to see her."

Jeanette said, "We get to ride on the double-decker bus."

I said, "I don't care."

She answered, "Mother Superior told me we both have to go to Newton Abbot to visit Mum."

I said, "She is your Mum, not mine."

"Okay, Maidy," she said. "Do this for our brother, Chris. You want to see him don't you?"

"I don't want to see the new sister or her father, but I want to see my brother," I replied.

Shirley and Ellen were standing beside me and said, "You want to see your brother and you are with your sister. It will be okay."

Jeanette said, "I put the clothes on your bed you will wear visiting Mum."

"What time do we leave?" I asked.

She said, "Wear your new clothes to mass and we will leave after breakfast."

Ellen, Shirley and I went into the dining room for breakfast. I tried to eat my bread and jam, but felt a lump in my throat thinking about the trip to Newton Abbot. I gave half of my sandwich to Ellen who was always hungry.

I saw Sister Teresa in the dining room and she looked right at me and came over to see me.

She said, "Mother Superior told me you are going to visit your mother."

"I don't want to see my mother, but I do want to see my brother," I replied.

"Everything will be just fine, and I know you will love the ride on the double decker-bus," she said

I told my friends I always felt much better after talking to Sister Teresa.

Ellen said, "She is your Baptismal God Mother and you're her pet."

"Sister Teresa is nice to everybody, but she watches out for you especially," said Shirley.

We wandered over to the library and picked up a sock each to darn while Mother Superior read a classic to us. The story took my mind off the upcoming trip.

That night I saw my new clothes placed at the end of the bed and I threw them on the floor and then kicked them under the bed. I felt angry, and I knew deep inside that it was not my fault, but why did I feel so guilty?

I knelt down by my bed and rested my head on the mattress. I prayed to Jesus to give me strength to face whatever I had to face tomorrow. I then sat on my bed and banged my head up and down against the wall for all the mean things I had said today. I tossed and turned during the night and got up to pee two or three times. I had to walk by Sister Teresa's room and I knew she heard me as the floorboards creaked outside her door. After I got back into bed, Sister came over to check on me, but I pretended to be asleep.

That night I could hear the piercing music of Beethoven from Sister Teresa's room. It was Beethoven's Fifth Symphony, which penetrated through my body and soul. Beethoven was my favorite because he was deaf.

He had a musical language of his own wrapped in piano notes that lingering within my soul. As the music played into the night, I breathed in the notes from the music sheet that floated before my eyes like angels. When the music stopped, the chords continued to play in my heart, giving me the time and space to take it all in and leave wanting more.

I gazed up at the long wooden beams in the ceiling and smiled, thinking of the time when I was swinging on them and Sister Teresa came out of her room to see if I had lost my mind. She turned me over on the bed and spanked my bottom. It didn't hurt that much, but it taught me that I could only do these antics when she was at Vespers. I fell asleep to be awakened by my classmates getting ready for mass. I dressed in the new yellow dress and a brown cardigan, but felt uncomfortable. The dress my mother had left for me was too big and it made me feel awkward, but I wore it to mass.

Shirley whispered to me during mass, "You look pretty in the color yellow."

I turned to Ellen and said, "It's too big, and it looks stupid on me."

She whispered, "You look like a buttercup, and the dress is pretty."

I said, "Thank you, Ellen. You know my favorite flower."

Mother Superior was sitting directly behind us and she started to cough which was the signal she was giving to us to stop talking.

My sister came to pick me up after breakfast and said, "Maidy, you look pretty in your new dress."

She was wearing a green dress, and I told her, "You look smashing!"

We left the convent and walked through the village to catch the double decker bus. Mother Superior gave us bus passes to give to the bus driver. When we arrived at the bus stop, I saw the bus coming towards us; I felt excited about the trip. We both climbed upstairs and found a seat at the front of the bus. Our first trip to Newton Abbot was the longest trip I had taken from Mary Church with my sister. We traveled down long winding country lanes, and I saw cows and sheep spread out on the green meadows chewing the grass. There were fields and fields of buttercups and daisies.

"Jeanette, let's get off the bus and run in the fields and pick as many butter cups that we can," I said.

She laughed and said, "Oh Maidy, you are so funny."

Our bus stopped near a farm with a crooked wooden fence to pick up farmers, and I saw some pigs in a pen. They looked like they had bathed in mud. As the bus turned the corner we passed a row of thatch roof cottages. I pressed my nose against the window, and I saw a bunch of chickens walking around the gardens.

It was a windy, cloudy day, and the bus made a rattling sound and a bumpity-bump going down the hill. When the bus got close to the oak trees, which were lined along a country lane, the long branches brushed up against the side of the bus, knocking on the window.

"Who's there?' I whispered.

Jeanette said, "The oak trees." We both laughed.

She said, "Maidy, I told you it would be fun."

"Riding the bus is exciting because you don't know which side you want to sit on, and you don't want to miss anything." I replied.

The bus finally drove into Newton Abbot bus station and my sister said, "I can see Mum. She is waiting for us."

Mum was dressed in a gray cotton dress and a blue sweater

with her long black hair dangling down her back, standing with a big smile on her face.

I said to Jeanette, "How can she look so happy after what she did to us?"

Jeanette answered, "Maidy, try to be a good girl for me and smile."

I did not feel like smiling at this woman who wanted to be our mother after she dumped us in an orphanage.

We climbed down off the bus and Mum came towards us and said, "Here are my two girls."

She hugged Jeanette and reached down to hug me but I froze. I did not want this woman touching me. I felt deep down she knew I would not be easy to be loved by her. I did not trust her. We walked across the street to her apartment, which was a walking distance from the bus station.

As we approached the front door of her home, I stopped and stood still. I felt a cold clammy hand grasping on me pulling me back. My feet were stuck to the ground. Suddenly I heard Jeanette's voice.

"Maidy, come on." She said. "Everyone is waiting for us."

I looked at her and said, "Okay I'm coming. Don't rush me."

We entered the front door and followed Mum into a bright yellow kitchen where a man and a young blonde girl were sitting at a table staring at us.

Mum pointed at the man and said, "This is Andrew, your new daddy."

I almost choked and said, "I have a daddy."

Both the man and girl glanced at me with a frown on their face, but nobody answered me. No one in this room could understand that I felt sick to my stomach. How I wished I could run back to Marychurch and leave this strange place. I know it is only a bad dream, but I just stood there defiantly.

The man nodded at us, ignoring my remark, and said, "Hello girls, welcome to the family."

I glared at him; he had a moon-shaped face with dark

brown eyes and a bushy mustache. He was wearing a fringe around his almost-bald head and spoke with a foreign accent. He was not English. Where was he from?

Mum was standing right near him like nothing had happened and said, "Girls, this is Barbara, your sister."

She giggled and then said, "Hello."

I was dumbfounded. I felt someone had sewn a zipper across my mouth. Why is this stupid girl giggling? She got up from her chair and stood beside me with a pink frilly dress and a big bow wrapped around a mess of curly hair, reminding me of one of the rich cousins in Jane Eyre. I looked at Jeanette, and she asked, "Where is our brother?"

Mum said, "Here he is."

A dark curly headed boy two years older than me walked in the room with a wide grin and said, "Hello, I'm Christopher."

I wondered if he looked like our Daddy.

Jeanette and I both said, "Hello."

I looked directly at my brother and said, "How long have you been home?"

He turned to Mum and said, "Mum, how long have I been home?"

She said, "A few years. But you went to St. Vincent, a boys' orphanage and it closed down after the war. Most of the refugees went back to London. I had to take you home."

I looked at my step-sister, Barbara, when she asked, "What is a refugee?"

"I am a refugee," I said.

Mum replied, "Maidy, you are not a refugee."

"I live in Marychurch," I said. "The village people and the kids who attended our school during the day call us refugees or orphans."

When we went to mass, I could hear whispers from the church members as we passed by their pews in a long procession, saying, "Here come the refugees from the war."

Mum looked straight at me with a scowl and raised eyebrows and said, "Enough! This discussion is over, Maidy."

I looked at Jeanette who put her finger on her lips, giving me a sign not to say any more about the refugees. I was angry at Mum, trying to dismiss it like nothing had happened, and we were all one big happy family. For my sister's peace of mind I said nothing more on the subject.

Jeanette was a peacemaker, and she had mothered me from the time I was born. She had a calmness about her that soothed me and could make me smile. When I was angry, Jeanette always knew the right words to say, and it made better sense when my mind was scrambled like eggs especially after my mother's visits. Jeanette loved to read and play the piano. She tried to protect me from mean people, but it was too overwhelming for her.

Suddenly my mother said, "Why don't we sit down and have some lunch. You must be hungry?"

I said, "I'm not hungry. I had a big breakfast at Marychurch." Nobody answered me.

Mum's husband, Andrew, said to my brother, "You sit between Jeanette and Maidy." Then he turned to Barbara, and said, "You sit on the other side of Maidy."

I sat down at the table and wished I could disappear. I felt so uncomfortable and looked at Jeanette, and I could see she was feeling scared of this new situation.

Mum served us spaghetti on toast for lunch, but I had to force the food into my mouth as I had an upset stomach and was not hungry. Barbara was five years younger than me, and I did not know what to say to her.

She said, "Maidy, did you like riding on the double-decker bus?"

I answered, "Yes, it was fun."

Barbara then chatted about the bus ride she has to take to school each day. I barely listened; I wanted this day to end. All I could think of was that foreign man would not be my father. I will not desert my father the way my mother did. Mum hardly mentioned his name, and if Jeanette or I did, she changed the subject. Every time I looked at him he was staring right back at me. He made me feel uneasy and that gut feeling never went away.

My brother interrupted my thoughts and said, "Maidy, you don't remember me since you were a baby the last time I saw you."

I said, "Jeanette told me about you, but we didn't know where you were living."

Mum interrupted. "Maidy, eat your spaghetti."

I said, "I am not hungry, and I am not eating anymore."

I looked at Jeanette and asked, "When are we going back home to Marychurch?"

She answered, "Maidy, we will visit Mum, and we will be back at Marychurch for Benediction."

Barbara asked, "What is Benediction?"

"Don't you know about Jesus?" I answered.

She stood in front of me with her hands on her hips and said, "You are a mean girl, and I don't want you to be my sister."

The stupid girl started to cry and ran in her room with her father walking behind her as he gave me a nasty look.

Mum said, "Maidy, your sister was very excited that she was getting two new sisters and has been waiting all morning for you. Please try to be patient with her."

I didn't answer; I sat at the table banging my knee up and down. Jeanette looked at me with a frown on her face and I glared back at her.

My brother broke the silence and suggested we play the game of Ludo. Barbara came back into the kitchen and the four of us played the board game together, and we let Barbara win at the request of my brother, whispering in my ear before the game, "Barbara is a bad loser and makes my life miserable when she loses a game."

I liked my brother as he smiled every time his eyes met

mine, and he told funny jokes during our games. I thought he was very good looking. Mum came into the kitchen and said, "It is time for you girls to catch your bus to Marychurch, and we will walk you over to the bus station."

I was so relieved when we finally said goodbye and got on the bus. My brother yelled, "Come back soon."

I waved goodbye and Mum blew us kisses. Jeanette blew kisses back but I didn't. We climbed upstairs on the bus and sat at the back as the seat in front was taken. Mum, Chris, and Barbara stood there waving until the bus left the square.

After the bus took off down the street. My sister turned and looked at me and said, "You were mean to Mum and Andrew."

I said, "I hate them. I especially hate that foreign man and his stupid daughter."

Jeanette said, "We can never go home, if you act mean to them, and I don't want to stay at Marychurch until I graduate from school."

I said, "You can go home when Mum gets a house, but I am not going with you."

Jeanette said. "You don't like Mum or Andrew, do you Maidy?"

I said, "That man is not English. Where is he from?"

"Christopher said he was Polish. I think Poland is in Europe near Germany." Jeanette answered.

I said, "Maybe he comes from Germany and is a friend of Hitler."

"No, Maidy. Remember our Daddy is from a foreign country."

I can remember Daddy's aunts coming to visit us at Marychurch and telling us the story about Daddy moving to England. In 1923, Daddy was seven years old and both the aunts had to go to Mexico and bring him back to England after his father died.

"Jeanette, don't ever, ever, compare that man to Daddy.

71

Hitler was not from Mexico. He came from Germany and is the reason why Daddy is dead."

We stayed quiet for the rest of the trip home. I looked out the window, and I wanted to yell at the cows and sheep. I wished I were an animal, then I would never have to speak to anybody.

The bus was bumping against the branches from the trees and Jeanette said, "Who is there?"

She looked at me and we both laughed. We arrived at Marychurch and got off the bus.

When we walked through the village Jeanette grabbed my hand and said, "I will always take care of you, and I know how upset you are, but please try for me. I want us to have a home that we belong in."

We both stopped walking and sat on a red brick wall close to the convent and cried. Jeanette said, "I hide my feelings; I have to be strong for both of us. I will never forgive Mum for what she did and I hate her, but thank God, Maidy, we have each other."

"Jeanette, I was a baby when I was left at Marychurch. These people are strangers. I hate them, but I feel something for my brother because he is part of Daddy. Andrew scares me, especially the way he stares at us."

Jeanette wiped my tears with her glove and said, "I love you, Maidy. And things will get better especially if we pray to the Virgin Mary, when we say the rosary."

I said, "I love you too Jeanette, but why did it take so long for Mum to come and see us?"

"I wish I knew the answer," she replied.

"My brother seems to love her, but he was not left at St Vincent as long as we have been left at Marychurch," I said.

Jeanette looked at me and said; "Maidy, we cannot crucify ourselves over Mum, because it is not our fault. She is the one that has to answer to Daddy when she dies."

I said, "Daddy will be so mad at her that she will have to live with that foreign man in Heaven."

We both laughed, and I looked up to the clouds and said, "Daddy, I hope you heard us. We love you Daddy."

Jeanette said, "He is like a shining star watching over us."

"Do you think that Heaven is real or make believe like Father Christmas?" I asked her.

She answered, "We know in our heart and soul there is a God, and God lives in a big home like Buckingham Palace, where the King of England lives. God calls his home Heaven, and he invites only good people who die, like Daddy, to live there with him."

I said, "Do you think he lets Daddy sit up on the clouds and watch us?"

Jeanette said, "I think that God keeps him close to us as we are his children and in our Bible class, Jesus said, "Suffer the little children come unto thee."

I said, "We have suffered enough because of Mum and the war."

Jeanette answered, "When I think of Mum and Dad, I get this pain in my heart. I have forgotten what they look like. I should have some memories about Daddy but I don't, and this makes me feel sick to my stomach."

"Jeanette, will this pain ever go away?" I asked.

She replied, "I hope so, but we need to pray to the Virgin Mother as she can tell Jesus how sad we both are and give us courage to move on with our lives."

"I will never ever forgive Mum for leaving us." I said in a loud voice. "She is a mean person."

"Come on, Maidy. We will be late for supper."

We both hugged each other and walked again through the gates of Marychurch.

There are so many wonderful memories I shared with my sister and friends.

I left Marychurch and walked towards the village to catch

my bus back to Exeter. I stopped by the brick wall and thought of my father's two dear old aunts that will stay in my heart for evermore. They came into my life at Marychurch, and made a difference through family unity.

Chapter 10

Visitors at Marychurch

I strolled through the village of Marychurch, with many mixed thoughts about my childhood. I stopped and sat down on a wooden bench outside the secondhand shop and pulled out a scrap of paper and pen. I wrote down my visits from my aunts, which were twice a month after the war, and definitely more than Mum's visits, which were monthly after she moved back from Norwich to Devon, where she lived with Andrew, Barbara and Christopher.

Aunty Ruby never came back to Marychurch after she and Mum dropped us off. Occasionally mum's sister Aunty Wilhelmina and Uncle Ken came and visited us and brought sweets and biscuits. This was after the war. They both were very nice and told Jeanette and I how much they loved and admired our father and missed him very much.

I remember my monthly visits from Aunt Susanna and Aunt Lucretia. They left me with many happy memories of times we spent together, especially as they were Daddy's relatives and told us many stories of his childhood, and showed us photos of my father growing up and in the Royal Air Force.

They kept these pictures in special family albums placed on the round cherry wood coffee table. The photo albums were big heavy flat books too heavy for Jeanette or I to hold. We would kneel on the rug by the table while the aunts took turns in turning the pages for us. The pages were black and felt like blotting paper we used in school. The aunts had attached the black and white shiny photos with white triangular corner stickers on each page. Jeannette and I dared not touch the photos with our hands, or our aunts would scold us

I remember touching one picture of Daddy after Aunt Lucretia told me not to touch it, and she slapped my hand and hit Daddy right on the face, leaving a smudge from my sweaty hand. I ran to the bathroom and sat on the toilet and cried.

I heard Aunt Susanna calling my name, but I ignored her. Then there was silence. I finally came out of the bathroom and went back to the living room and told my aunts, "I won't touch the pictures," and that I was sorry.

I do remember how much Jeanette and I enjoyed looking through the pictures, especially the ones of when he was a little boy growing up in Torreon, Mexico. There was one picture that the aunts said I looked like him and it was a picture of Daddy holding my grandpa's hand. He was wearing a wide brim hat.

My very favorite picture was a big one of Daddy in his uniform. This picture was on a white dresser in the bedroom my sister and I shared at my aunt's cottage. I can remember the first time I saw his picture.

I said to my sister, "Daddy is so handsome, and he is dark-looking like me."

Jeanette answered, "He looks like a movie star, and his smile lights up the room."

We both looked at each other, finally knowing what our father looked like, and we were not disappointed. From that day forward, when I looked up to the sky I would call out to my father, "I can see you Daddy."

If I looked really hard, I could see his face in the clouds smiling back at me. Each time we spent the night at the cottage, the first thing I did was run into the bedroom and kiss my father's picture. Sometimes when my sister was helping Aunt Susanna with the dishes in the kitchen, I would lie on my bed with his framed picture clutched to my heart. I told him repeatedly how much I loved him and missed him. Sometimes we giggled when I told him about his aunts being strict.

"Oh Daddy," I said, "they tell us so many wonderful stories, especially about Grandpa and you in Mexico." I loved the story when Daddy hid the mushy peas in his trouser pocket, and Aunt Susanna found them when she was doing laundry.

Aunt Lucretia said, "He hated peas and brussel sprouts. I spanked your father for wasting food, and I will do the same with you girls if you ever do such a thing."

I am like you, Dad, because I did not like mushy peas or brussels when I was young, but I grew to love them when I went to nursing school. I would eat them late at night after coming home from a date. They were cold and yummy right from the tin.

When I held his picture I would trace my fingers around his face and stare at him. I asked him about the aunts praying like nuns all day Saturday.

I told him they were very religious. "Not Catholics," I said. "God is the same, but their preacher is married and he can have children. Our priest is married to the church. Daddy, this is hard for me to understand."

Jeanette and I had to pray and listen to stories from the Bible and go to church with them on Saturday at the Christian Scientist Church.

I tried to picture Daddy growing up very religious with all those prayers and spending all day in the church on Saturday.

"Daddy," I said, "I told you about the beautiful cottage garden and how it was my favorite place. I loved every inch of it. Especially the flowers blooming in many colors spread all over the garden."

I felt sad when I had to say goodbye to my father because I actually believed he was in the picture. I nodded my head as I looked back remembering kissing the glass-framed picture every time I entered the bedroom.

My elderly aunts took great pride in their home. I watched them shake their couch pillows every time Jeanette and I sat on them. They did not like dirty dishes left in the sink. The aunts knitted their long skirts and sweaters and had a big basket of knitting wool and metal knitting needles in the corner of the living room. The colors were assorted but mainly dark brown and light brown. They made sweaters for my sister and me in dark navy blue to match our school uniforms.

Daddy's father was my aunts' brother. After the death of my grandfather, my aunts went to Torreon, Mexico and brought my father back to England and adopted him as their son. He was seven years old, and they sent him to Rugby, a boarding school for boys. When he graduated from Rugby, he went to University of London and worked part time as the headwaiter at The Clarence House in London.

This was the hotel where he met and hired my mother as a food server in May 1936. She had dropped out of nursing school and was five months pregnant with my sister Jeanette. I was visiting Uncle Mick in Exeter when I was in nursing school, and he told me about my parents' love story.

He said, "Your mother was beautiful with big green eyes and long raven black hair. She looked like a Spanish movie star. When she walked into the dance hall with me, everybody, especially the men, turned and looked at her. My Uncle told me that my father fell madly in love with her the first time he met her. He did not mention the pregnancy, and I did not find out about my sister being my half sister until a much later time in my late thirties, when my brother told me.

When war broke out in 1939, Daddy joined the Royal Air Force and was a member of the 103 Black Swan Squadron who flew dangerous missions over Belgium and Germany to defeat the enemy. Both his aunts were upset about the war as they were both strict Christian Science and did not want my father to go into the military. It was against their religion, and they did not believe in the bloodshed caused by war, even if it was to defend the country. My father joined the Royal Air Force because he did not want to be known as a conscientious objector. I remember one time when we were walking home from the church I asked the aunts, "Why did Daddy join the Air Force?"

Aunt Lucretia said, "Your father was pressured into joining the service. Your mother's three brothers had already joined up, and they were nagging him to volunteer his service."

"They bullied him at the pub into joining the service, and your mother did nothing to stop it!" said Aunt Susanna. "He joined at the University of London without our knowledge."

My aunts didn't like my mother and did not want her to put us in Marychurch. Aunt Susanna said they wanted to adopt my brother and me, but my mother would not let that happen. "Why not Mum?" I wondered. "You didn't want us girls!"

Sometimes I wish the aunts had adopted us, but I would have been separated from my sister Jeanette, and that would have been a great loss in my life. My aunts were in their late sixties when Jeanette and I were at Marychurch.

Aunt Susanna was slight in build and her narrow face was serene with gentleness. She had big brown soft eyes and wore thick spectacles. Her gray brown hair was pinned up in a bun at the back of her head.

Aunt Lucretia was taller and thinner than her sister. She had a stern face and piercing green eyes. When she spoke to you, she looked right through you. She wore her gray hair in a tight bun at the back of her head and carried her glasses on a chain around her neck. Aunt Lucretia was five years older than Aunt Susanna. Both aunts dressed like characters from the Charles Dickens era. They wore long thick hand-knitted skirts, silk or satin blouses, felt hats with feathers that sat on the back of their heads, and dark brown laced-up shoes with thick brown stockings covering their legs. They both walked with crooked carved wooden walking canes with silver polished handles. Often they would poke their sticks at my sister and me as we were crossing the country lanes.

With a smile, I stopped to get on the double-decker bus to go back to Exeter where I was staying. On my bus ride, I realized Aunt Lucretia made most of the household decisions, which we all followed. Both aunts were strict in their religious beliefs, which was instilled in my sister and I when we spent time with them at the cottage. I told Jeanette in one day we said more prayers from morning until night than we did at Marychurch all week.

The aunts woke us up each morning. We put on our thick knitted dressing gowns, and followed them into the living room, keeling down in front of the fireplace. Aunty Susanna would read the morning prayers. After prayers we went to the bathroom, and washed our face and brushed our teeth. We dressed in the clothes the aunts made for us, which stayed at the cottage. Aunt Lucretia would brush and plait our hair, putting colorful ribbons on the ends of our pig-tails.

Afterwards, we sat in the kitchen at a small table covered with a green or red checkered table cloth. It was neatly set with bone china bowls and plates covered with a pretty violet pattern. The silverware was set on a cloth napkin beside the breakfast bowl.

After they poured the porridge into the bowls, both aunts sat down with us, and we prayed together to thank God for our food. I remember their morning prayers were much longer than ours at Marychurch. When I told the aunts the prayers were different from the ones we said at Marychurch, Aunt Lucretia said, "You are supposed to be practicing our religion. It is only because your mother put you at Marychurch that you practice Catholicism."

Aunt Susanna said, "Your father was raised a Christian Scientist, and he would want you to respect his beliefs by attending church on the Sabbath, which is Saturday."

Jeanette answered, "We don't mind, do we Maidy?"

"I do mind! Because we spend all day there, and I would rather be here playing with my doll."

Aunt Lucretia looked directly at me and said, "Young lady, we all have one God, and there are many religions. When you are staying with me, you will practice the Christian Science religion, and attend the service on the Sabbath day."

The bus was rocking up and down as we went down a narrow winding lane, and I continued to smile as we passed special places that Jeanette and I had been with the aunts when we were young girls.

I looked out the left window of the bus as we danced down the country lane where birds chirped and built their nests in the spreading chestnut trees, which formed an arch across the lane and shaded out the sun. When the bus pulled into the Exeter station, I got off and walked across the street to the hotel.

Chapter 11

God Loves You Just the Way You Are — Nogales Cottage

It was springtime in England, and I could hear the screeching sounds of the seagull from the ocean.

After eating breakfast at the hotel, I started off my morning walk to the bus station. I wanted to go back to Shiphay Lane and see Nogales Cottage before going back to America.

My aunts named their cottage after a town our Mexican family lived in Mexico. I felt a strong urge to walk down the country lane to see the yellow primroses and buttercups dancing in the green fields and watch the daffodils swaying with the gentle winds. My two old aunts were long gone, and they had left the cottage to the Christian Scientist church. Mum tried to change the will through a court attorney but to no avail. The will was legal, and she got nothing.

When I arrived at the bus station, there was a bus waiting. I got on the bus and told the driver to drop me off on Shiphay Lane. The bus started to go bumpity, bumpity as it went through the village. I sat in front on the top deck of the bus and thought about my two aunts picking my sister and me up from Marychurch to take us to the cottage for the weekend. Friday morning was our pick up day, and they would bring us back to Marychurch Sunday afternoon.

My aunts fetched us in a black Bentley car, which was driven by a driver from the Christian Scientist Church who took us to Nogales on Shiphay lane near Cockington village.

The cottage was white with a thatched roof and had a white picket fence. I remember the white lace curtains drawn back in the bay windows as Jeanette and I were forbidden to touch them. Aunt Lucretia said, "Your hands are not clean."

I loved the dark brown front door of the cottage as it looked like a big chocolate bar with a shiny gold doorknob. The brass letterbox on the door made it appear that the door had a big mouth..

When you walked into the front garden, there were lots of sweet smelling flowers nestled all around the picket fence and in the center was a circle of white gravel which led a pathway to the front door with red and pink English tea roses nestling on either side. I often stopped to smell the scent of the roses and loved picking up loose petals. I remember when I was walking on the white gravel and hearing that crunchy sound made from my Clarks school shoes.

The back garden was full of fruit trees, and there was a large vegetable patch with rows of cabbages, potatoes and cauliflowers. I smelled the sprouts, which were clinging to their long stalks in the corner of the garden. I could not see the potatoes, which were planted in the back garden deep in a rich reddish dirt. When they were ready to be dug up my aunt would let Jeanette and me help her. I loved squishing my hands in the rich dirt. Aunty would make me rinse my hands off under the water tap located outside their greenhouse before going back to the cottage.

There were blackberry bushes behind two apple trees that secured the clothesline, where my aunts hung their clean washing. Sparrows perched themselves on the branches and chirped beautiful sounds, especially in the early morning.

At the back of the garden was a chestnut tree, which spread over an old wooden shed. Close by was a tree stump, and I would sit there and watch the red squirrels scurry up and down the tree onto the shed roof. I loved to hear their pitter-patter noise from their feet.

In the center of the garden was a cement bird bath filled with water nestled by a spray of planted lavender, expelling a beautiful scent around the garden. I would stand close to the lavender, and watch the birds taking a bath. It was fun to see them splash in the water, which sprayed in the air from their wings. I loved this garden and called it my "secret garden." It was a place I could go and find peace by watching God's creations..

Jeanette and I spent many hours in the garden. This was the home where Daddy grew up with his father's sisters, whom he loved dearly.

An old wooden swing in the garden belonged to my father, and I would often sit on the swing, and read my books pretending I was sitting on my father's lap. Whenever the aunts saw me on the swing they would say, "Your daddy loved that swing."

On Saturday my sister and I wore our best dresses that were kept in the wooden closet in our bedroom. There were two beds dressed with yellow-flowered canopies that we slept in. We felt like two princesses. Our dolls would sit on our bed. Our bedroom window faced the back garden and when I lay on my bed in the early morning, I watched the birds fluttering in the branches of the fruit trees. I wished that I could stay with my aunts and never go back to Marychurch. Whenever I asked the aunts to keep Jeanette and me with them, it was the same answer, "Your mother wouldn't hear of such a thing."

Aunt Lucretia said, "Maidy, you and your sister would have to change religion from Catholic to Christian Science." I told her I didn't care. We could not play in the garden during the early part of the day as my aunts did not want us to disturb the neighbors with our idle chatter. Jeanette and I would wait until after our lunch when most neighbors had gone inside their homes or were out shopping. During the day we played with our hand knitted doilies that Aunt Susanna made for us with two different outfits. Jeanette called her doll Tilly, and I called mine Tolly.

Friday was a fun day as the Aunts baked bread, pies, cakes, and ginger men biscuits. The cooking was done on a kitchen range. On one side of the range was a boiler which heated the water and on the other side was an oven for baking. There was a fireplace in the middle of the range where logs were burnt to make it hot. We had to wait nearly two hours before the oven was hot enough to do the baking and that was the time for the preparation of the baked goods.

Jeanette and I spent the morning in the kitchen helping our aunts. We had to wear our red checkered aprons and wash our hands. I stirred the cake mixture with Aunt Susanna, and Jeanette helped Aunt Lucretia roll out the pastry.

Aunt Susanna said, "You and Jeanette can have the leftover biscuit dough and make something for yourselves while your aunt and I wash dishes."

This was the fun part as Jeanette and I made two dolls and dipped them in brown sugar. Aunt Lucretia saw me put some dough in my mouth, which I had dipped in the brown sugar, and rushed over to me and said, "Don't do that again young lady or you will stay out of the kitchen."

"I'm sorry," I said. "I like the taste of it."

She answered, "You like the taste of the brown sugar?"

Aunt Susanna smiled and said, "Let me put some raisin eyes on your dolls and when they come out of the oven, I will make them a pink dress with icing."

Jeanette said, "Look, Maidy. The dolls are ready. Thank you Aunt Susanna."

Aunt Susanna smiled and popped them into the oven to bake

We were not allowed to touch the baked goods for the church, but we prayed over them twice on Friday. Sugar was rationed, and it was important to take food to the church for people that were less fortunate than us. My aunts baked Jeanette and me two gingerbread men.

On Saturday, their holy day, we prayed in the early morning asking for God's blessing over the food for the church and giving thanks for our oatmeal for breakfast. Jeanette and I had a bath in a tin bath that Aunt Susanna brought into the kitchen so we could stay warm. After our baths we dressed in our best clothes left out by Aunt Lucretia on our beds.

At 9:00 in the morning the Aunts walked with us over to their church, which was a mile away, and we all carried bread, pastries and fruit in string bags for their Christian Science Church.

As we were walking, my aunts said, "You girls need to think of our pastor somewhat like your priest."

I said to Aunties, "Your pastor is married with four children, and our priest is married to the Virgin Mary."

Jeanette laughed out loud and said, "No Maidy, they are not married to the Virgin Mary, because she had a husband called Joseph."

I said, "I know Jeanette, but the priest cannot get married to a woman."

Aunt Susanna said, "Maidy, do not ask the pastor why he is married, and do not discuss the priest at our church."

Aunt Lucretia said, "You girls do not discuss Marychurch or any of our personal business to anyone you meet at the church today. If anyone has any questions, tell them to come and see me."

"Yes, we understand you," each of us said.

We stayed at the church for four hours. After the long service we had to visit with the pastor and all the church people. We sat down in the church hall close to our aunts and had a drink of lemonade and a scone with strawberry jam. My aunts talked to every person that passed us, and Jeanette and I just sat there bored to tears. I asked Aunt Susanna if I could eat another scone and she said in a whisper, "No, Maidy, you have had enough, and you need to leave space for afternoon tea."

Jeanette and I listened to the aunts talking about the war, food rationing and why Mrs. Spencer and her children weren't at prayer service. I nudged Jeanette and said, "Who cares?'

Jeanette said, "We will be leaving soon. I heard Aunt Lucretia asking about the pastor."

I said, "If she gets talking with him we will be here forever." Jeanette said, "Here comes the pastor."

He greeted us with a warm welcome, and Jeanette and I sat on the bench, with a watchful eye from Aunt Lucretia.

The aunts talked with the pastor, for a short time, regarding church business. We finally left the church and started our walk back to Nogales Cottage.

The country lanes were quite narrow, and when a car passed by we had to walk in single file. The aunts made Jeanette and I walk in front. If we didn't move fast enough, we would get a poke with their cane. I thought it was funny as it never hurt me. When I was happy, I would skip along the lane with Jeanette, and occasionally when the horses were close to the lane grazing the aunts would let us pet them.

I loved walking past the thatch roof cottages. In the spring I would watch the workman re-thatching the roof at my Aunt's cottage until they would tell me to run along, since I asked too many questions. There were so many fun things to do at the cottage, especially at the time of year when Jeanette and I would help our aunts replant the garden. Their gardener kept a close eye on us to make sure we did not put the seeds of the vegetables down too deep in the dirt.

During our walks, Aunty Lucretia pointed out the small buds on the willow tree with her walking cane, and I watched them burst out into catkins by the end of spring. You could smell the strong scent of honeysuckle which draped over the bushes on each side of the country lane. I loved walking back and forth to the church. There was always something new and breathtaking to see. I would stop and watch the cows and sheep in the nearby fields grazing amongst the buttercups and daisies. It was fun to see chickens that scratched and clucked as you passed them by.

Aunt Susanna said, "Life is a gift from God."

Jeanette said, "Why can't animals speak?"

I chimed in and said, "Jeanette, animals do speak. The cows moo, the sheep baa, and dogs bark. These sounds show you the animal's emotions."

Aunt Lucretia said, "Animals are also a gift from God for food and companionship."

I said, "I don't want to eat the animals because that will hurt them."

Jeanette answered, "Maidy, we eat rabbit stew at Marychurch and you like stew."

I said, "I never think of a rabbit when I eat the stew, but I will now."

Aunt Lucretia walked much slower than Aunt Susanna, and when I walked with her she asked me about school.

She said, "Maidy, education is very important, and you must study hard at school."

I said, "Aunty, I have good grades, and I like school."

She said, "Your father was a smart student, and he was a good boy growing up with your Aunt and I."

I said, "Do you miss Daddy as much as I do?'

I watched her pull a handkerchief out of her purse and dab her eyes.

She stopped and looked at me sadly and said, "I loved your father so much and miss him. There is not a day that goes by that I don't think of him, and when I see you I see him in your eyes and your smile."

I squeezed her hand, and we continued walking, knowing how special this time was we spent together. When we arrived at the cottage Jeannette and I went to our bedroom to relax since both aunties were ready to take their afternoon nap.

I walked down the lane and passed by the cottage. I stopped and blew a kiss for some of the most wonderful memories of my childhood. I crossed the lane and went down to the ocean and walked along the sand.

I could hear the screeching sound of the seagulls and smell the seaweed strewn all over the beach. I picked some up and loved the rubbery feel between my fingers. I washed it in the ocean and tasted the salty green seaweed. I threw it back into the ocean and smiled recapping the times I had walked on this beach with my brother and sisters. My walks with the aunts were memories of collecting shells, which they spread around some of their green plants.

The aunts also bought us ice cream, and we sat on the sand to enjoy them and watch the small boats in the ocean. Jeanette and I built sand castles in the sand and for those moments we were both fairy princesses who lived in a castle with a king and queen.

I stopped and picked up three pebbles and threw one after the other in the ocean, looked up to the sky and said, *"This is for you, Jeanette and Aunties."*

Chapter 12

Tea with Aunt Lucretia
and Aunt Susanna

Whenever I returned to Devon, I would take the train to Torquay and have afternoon tea at the cafe on the top floor of Debenhams Department Store, overlooking the High Street. I remember the teas that Jeanette and I had shared with our aunts.

At four o'clock on a Sunday afternoon, we joined the aunts in the living room and knelt down in front of the brick fireplace and prayed for peace and for our souls. After prayers, the gardener drove us in my aunts' Bentley to a posh restaurant that was above Debenhams.

At teatime they seated us at a special table reserved for my aunts who came here quite often. The waiter pushed my dining room chair to the table as it was too heavy for me to move. Our tea was served on silver trays with dainty cucumber and egg salad sandwiches. They served our teacakes on a beautiful teared china plate. In the background, I could hear beautiful classical music. I remember asking Aunt Susanna if that was Tchaikovsky, and she said, "Yes, it was the music of Swan Lake."

Aunt Lucretia looked at me with a big smile and said, "Maidy, how did you know that was Tchaikovsky?"

I said, "Because at Marychurch, Sister Teresa played classical music at night in the dormitory. One night I asked her who the composer was, and it was Tchaikovsky."

"You are smart like your daddy," she said. "He loved classical music and took piano lessons when he was going to Rugby school."

"Rugby school?" I said. "Did he play rugby?"

Aunt Susanna laughed and said, "Yes, your daddy played rugby and his school was named after the rugby ball, because it is made in the little village surrounding the school."

Jeanette said, "I take piano lessons."

I said, "Jeanette can play God Save the King."

Aunt Susanna said, "Who teaches you Jeanette?"

She answered, "Mother Superior."

The teatime was a big thrill for my sister and me, eating in a posh restaurant and people waiting on us like we were two rich kids. I often wondered what it would have been like if my aunts had adopted me. I know that I would not be a Catholic; I would be Christian Science, and at this moment it sounded brilliant to me if this was the way I could live all the time.

Whenever Jeanette and I were with the Aunts, they always corrected us on our manners in the dining room at a restaurant. We had to place our big cloth napkins on our laps, and use the right utensils when we ate our food. We could not interrupt a conversation when another person was speaking. I remember a white-laced china bowl sitting on the table with brown sugar lumps for our tea. One time I picked out a sugar lump with my fingers and Aunt Susanna said, "Maidy, if you do that again, I will take you to the bathroom and spank you."

I said, "I'm sorry. I will use the spoon."

But I do remember getting a spanking for licking off the pink icing on one of the tea cakes and putting it back on the tray, and picking up a chocolate one which was snatched from my hand and placed on Jeanette's plate.

Aunt Lucretia said, "Maidy, come with me."

She took me to the bathroom, pulled down my knickers and slapped my bottom and said, "Don't you ever do that again!"

I remember, I didn't cry. Her slap was a tap compared to the ones the nuns at Marychurch gave us. My aunts were strict with us, but I know they loved me and missed my father.

Jeanette said after one of our visits, "Maidy, the aunts pay more attention to you than to me and seem more interested in your school work than mine."

I answered, "That is silly. It is probably because I am the youngest and need more attention."

But as I grew older, I could see I got nearly all the attention, and at that time I did not understand why.

On our next visit when the Aunts asked me about school, I said, "Jeanette won a music award."

The aunts looked at Jeanette and Aunt Susanna said, "That is very nice dear."

I said, "Jeanette is very smart, and she can play tennis better than I can."

Both aunts looked at Jeanette and nodded their heads and smiled. I was beginning to understand what Jeanette said, regarding the aunts paying more attention to me than her. The aunts were pleasant to my sister, but they were much more attentive to my needs.

After my tea, I got on the bus outside the department store and skirted through the old neighborhood. I look back over my childhood, and remember the time we spent with my aunts. I am older now and know that Jeanette was my half-sister, and Daddy had adopted her as his daughter.

Daddy was attending the University of London during the day and at night he worked at the Clarence hotel in the heart of London, as the head waiter. He hired my mother as a part-time waitress, knowing she was pregnant. After working together for a few weeks, they fell in love, even though Daddy knew about the baby. Within three months they got married in a registry office. It was a month before Jeanette was born on

September 27, 1936 in a London hospital. The aunts believed the baby belonged to my father, but against my mother's wishes, he told his aunts the truth when he joined the Air force.

I loved Jeanette. In my heart she was my beloved sister, and when she died with cancer at age thirty-nine, part of me died with her, leaving me with unfulfilled dreams that we had made together.

Jeanette, you should be sitting on this bus with me visiting our childhood memories together.

The pain of losing you lingers in my heart. But I know deep within, we will meet again, in a much better place where music plays on a piano by you, and birds sing, and the angels are all around you.

Chapter 13

When You Feel Like Giving Up, Try, Try, Again

The following day I took the bus to the Christian Science Church, in Torquay that my aunts attended. I walked into the church grounds around the parking area, which was empty. I climbed up the three steps to the church front door and turned the brass doorknob. The door was locked, with a long dead rusty bolt with a large padlock. I walked around the back of the church and wandered to the side door, and it was locked. The place was deserted.

There was a green wooden bench under a willow tree, and I sat down. My thoughts were churning. I was thinking about the war and the sacrifices people had to make during that time.

My Aunt Susanna was a newspaper reporter during World War II. She avidly followed the news around the world. I thought about the war stories she told Jeannette and me in their cottage around the fireside on a Saturday evening. I remember asking her about the London Blitz and telling the aunts that my two best friends, Shirley and Ellen, lost their parents in the bombings.

Aunt Lucretia said, "Do you know anything about the air raids?"

Jeanette answered, "We were attacked from the sky by the Germans and they dropped bombs everywhere."

My aunt replied, "Well done, Jeanette!"

"Tell the girls the story, Susanna." Aunt Lucretia said.

As the Aunts sat in their wooden rocking chairs, we sat on the warm rug close to the fireside, and Aunt Susanna told us the story of the London Blitz.

"Germany declared war on England on September 3, 1939, and air raids did not begin until September 7, 1940. This was when 300 German planes flew over London dropping bombs everywhere. Night after night the Germans came, putting the city in sheer terror. This was known as the London Blitz. Air-raid shelters and gas masks were issued to everyone to protect the people from poison gas during the air raids."

Aunt Lucretia said, "Maidy, your father was fighting the enemy during the London Blitz."

"He was so brave," I replied.

"Every time we had a drill at school, the nuns made us put the gas mask on our face, and I got an upset stomach with the smell of rubber," Jeanette said.

"What happened to all the children in the London Blitz?" I asked

Aunt Lucretia said, "The government moved them to safer places in the countryside where we live. They were transferred overseas to Canada, Australia, and New Zealand for their safety. Children who lost their parents went to places like Marychurch like your friends, Maidy. Everyone was given a national identity card so that they could prove who they were. It was a precaution designed to make it harder for enemy spies to operate in England."

"We don't have these cards, do we Jeanette?" I replied.

Jeanette said, "Yes we do, but Mother Superior has them in her office, and when we leave Marychurch we will be given the cards."

Aunt Lucretia said, "You also have ration books."

"I know, Aunty, because every time I leave food on my plate I get a lecture from Mother Superior complaining about food shortage, for many people who don't have enough food," I said.

Aunt Susanna asked Jeanette and I if we knew about the clothes ration book?

Jeanette and I both answered, "No."

I said, "How do you buy clothes with a ration book?"

"Clothes ration books started in 1941 because new clothes were scarce. The government issued each person a clothing book, and I am sure your mother has yours," said Aunt Lucretia.

"She never told us about the book, and I am sure she used the coupons on her clothes," I said.

Jeanette answered, "We don't know for sure, Maidy."

I looked at my sister and frowned at her.

Aunty Lucretia continued to tell us the ration book had 66 coupons for the whole year. A new coat would cost fifteen coupons and its value in money. To help overcome the worst shortages, there was a utility scheme introduced in 1941 to produce a range of useful items at low cost. Someone called them utility goods. These items were well made but plain, and little choice of style or color. Most people endured rationing because no one could afford to throw anything away. People would rip the yarn from old sweaters and knit many other items for their families.

I looked up to the sky and could see the dark clouds gathering together. I knew the rain was coming. I got up from the bench and took one look at the church.

"Goodbye, Aunty Lucretia and Aunt Susanna," I said aloud. "I love you dearly and thank you for the part we shared during my childhood."

As I walked back to catch my bus the rain was coming down fast. I zipped up my jacket and pulled my hood over my head. I was happy because I realized that whatever happens in your life there is a lesson to learn.

Writing my book has helped me understand that people who touch your pathway during your life came for a reason, and you will understand why when they say "Goodbye."

Chapter 14

My Beloved Sister Jeanette

I woke up to the morning sunrise shining brightly through my hotel window. I lay in bed staring at the white ceiling, and all I could think of was Jeanette, my sister, and our childhood.

Where have these years gone?

It seems like yesterday we were at Marychurch orphanage, going to mass in the morning and scurrying through our school days. Jeanette was more than just my sister. *She had replaced my mother.* Jeanette watched over me and guided me during my early childhood. She listened to me, and we prayed together.

Jeanette was a devout Catholic and believed the bible was a book written by God himself. I believed whatever my sister told me, especially about God.

Jeanette said, "Maidy, you must pray to the Virgin Mary when you need something special as she was Jesus's mother and Jesus would grant all her requests."

I gently touched my silver cross hanging from the chain around my neck, and prayed, "Oh Jesus, thank you for the gift of my sister. Please take care of her soul and cradle it with love."

I swung off my bed, got dressed, and left the hotel to catch the red double decker-bus to Marychurch.

On my way to the bus station, I stopped by the bakery and bought myself two sausage rolls and a cream bun. I stuffed the cream bun in my mouth, enjoying the sugary taste before the bus arrived. The bus was on time and I sat in the front. The wheels began to turn, and in the distance I could hear the church bells chiming from Exeter Cathedral. This was my favorite time of the year, the Christmas season. The bus drove through the village, and I looked at the shops lit up with their decorations spread everywhere. I thought about the many Christmases I had enjoyed with my sister and friends at Marychurch.

I remember how excited my friends and I were when the first day of November came as this was the beginning of the Holy holidays. I could feel the magic in the air as we prepared for the birth of Jesus.

One Christmas my sister Jeanette worked in the kitchen helping the nuns preparing Christmas puddings, cakes, biscuits and pies for the holiday season. This was a privilege given to senior students who excelled in subjects during the school year. She was thirteen and I was nine years old and she got me a job as her assistant.

My friends Shirley and Ellen were so jealous, but I made them feel better when I brought back some baked goods that I had squashed in my pocket.

Jeanette and I had so much fun together working in the kitchen, especially when we rolled out the pastry for the fruit pies with a heavy wooden rolling pin that had a handle on each end.

Sister Margaret showed us how to roll out the pastry. She said, "Girls, put plenty of flour on your rolling pin so it does not stick to the pastry, and you can get a smooth surface by slowly rolling the pastry back and forth with your hands firmly wrapped around the handles."

Jeannette would say, "Maidy, I love the smell of the kitchen when the fruit pies come out of the oven as they give off a sweet smell from the cinnamon."

"The best job is icing the biscuits," I said, "and being able to put some in my big apron pocket and take them to Shirley and Ellen."

Jeanette answered, "You better not let Sister Margaret catch you because she will send you out of the kitchen, and your baking days will be over."

The nuns made the Christmas pudding and Christmas cakes. When the puddings were boiled they were put in gauze cloth and tied up with string, and hung on a line in the large pantry next door to the kitchen. Every other day someone sprayed them with fruit juice from the apples, which came from the convent gardens.

Six Christmas cakes were put on a rack in the pantry and stayed there for a couple of days and then brought back in the kitchen to be iced and decorated. Sister Margaret had us all gather around the big wooden table to assist with the cake decorating.

Sister had a bowl of marzipan, made from almonds, margarine and eggs. She stirred it with a wooden spoon to make a smooth paste and spread it on the cakes. She said, "Girls, this is the foundation before icing."

Two girls were mixing the icing sugar with margarine and drops of lemon juice. I asked Sister Margaret, "Why do you put lemon juice in the icing?"

Sister said, "It preserves the icing as white as snow."

It was fun to learn about the Christmas cakes. There were two girls at each cake, and I was assisting Sister Margaret to spread the icing. She did half the cake, and I did the other half under her watchful eye.

Sister checked the other cakes and said, "Well done, girls. We will now ice the cake by spreading the icing on the cake like the marzipan. Then we will use a fork and swirl it around so the icing peaks up looking like snow."

After we finished, Sister was pleased with the results, and said, "We will now decorate the cake with three ornaments from the tray in the middle of the table."

Sister Margaret looked at me and said, "Maidy, you pick out the decorations and place them on the cake you and I were working on." I picked out a little handmade wooden house, a Christmas tree and a wooden Father Christmas. They looked like they came out of a Charles Dickens book.

I showed them to my sister Jeanette, and she smiled and said, "Good choice, Maidy." I placed the ornaments very carefully in the center of the cake. I stepped back and had a long look at my work and was very proud of myself.

Sister nodded her head and smiled at me from across the kitchen and told us girls what a great job we had done today. She gave us a rosy red apple to take back with us to the convent. I shared mine with Shirley and Ellen.

Memories of my sister and me are both joyful and painful. We had made so many plans for our future at Marychurch. One of these plans was to return here together as adults, but here I am sitting on this bus alone, feeling sorry for myself.

I looked out the bus window watching rain trickle down

leaving a faint mist on the window. The tree branches brushed up against the bus.

We drove down the lane towards Marychurch. Suddenly I smiled thinking of Jeanette saying who's there when the tree branches knocked against the window and I would answer, "It's the whispering willow tree saying, I want to go home."

When we passed the village grocery store, I could see the Christmas puddings stacked up in the window reminding me of Marychurch. I smiled thinking of the puddings hanging up on a line in the big larder and the night my friends, Shirley, Ellen and I found the kitchen unlocked.

We sneaked into the kitchen as Shirley looked back at me and said, "I will get some bread and cheese, and we can make some sandwiches."

Ellen replied, "I will look for the ginger biscuits."

I chimed in and said, "I am going to take a Christmas pudding since I helped them make it. The pudding will keep for a long time."

Shirley said, "You wouldn't dare!"

I replied, "Just watch me."

We all giggled.

We left the kitchen carrying our food wrapped in our school sweaters, feeling very proud of ourselves. The nuns were in church so we saw no one walking around as we went back to our dormitory.

Most of the girls in the dorm saw us and asked us what we had wrapped in our sweaters. We unfolded our sweaters on the beds and everyone saw our hidden treasure. They came running towards us, and we shared the pudding and biscuits with our dormitory friends. There was no Christmas pudding left.

The next morning as I entered through the kitchen door with my sister, I noticed the kitchen staff and the girls from the orphanage were lined up in front of the big pantry. Sister

Margaret was talking to them in a stern voice. Jeanette and I joined the group and sister looked directly at Jeanette and said,

"We have a thief amongst us, and I intend to find out which one of you took a Christmas pudding and some ginger biscuits from this kitchen."

"Sister, when did this happen?" I asked.

She said, "It happened in the late evening. I sprayed six puddings before Benediction. There was a tray of fresh-baked ginger biscuits. When I came in this morning I found all of them gone."

Jeanette squeezed my hand and whispered, "Please tell me you had nothing to do with the missing pudding, Maidy."

"Why do you think I had something to do with it?" I asked.

Sister Margaret coughed and looked right at Jeanette and said, "You two stop talking."

All I could think of was Shirley, Ellen, and some girls from our dormitory last night sharing the Christmas pudding resulting with an upset stomach the next morning, but we had a big giggle over our adventure in the kitchen.

Sister Margaret told us to work on the bread dough and knead the loaves that had been prepared on the table.

When we were all gathered around the big wooden table she said, "I expect someone to return the pudding tomorrow, or there will be consequences for all of you."

That evening when we were getting ready to leave the kitchen, Sister Margaret stopped me at the front door and said, "Young lady, I need to talk to you."

I asked Sister if Jeanette could stay and she said, "No, you can see your sister back at the convent."

After everybody had left Sister Margaret asked me to step into her office. She sat down, and I stood in front of her desk wishing the floor would split open so I could fall between the cracks.

Sister broke the silence with a statement. "Maidy, I know you had something to do with the missing pudding and biscuits, so don't spend time weaving stories. Two of your friends are with the doctor as we speak. They got sick eating too much Christmas pudding last night."

I looked straight at sister and said, "Who told you I gave them the pudding?"

"Never mind who told me, but they sleep in your dormitory." Sister scowled.

I burst out, "I took the pudding and the ginger biscuits!"

Sister said, "Did you know you broke the Sixth Commandment of God? Thou shalt not steal."

I answered, "The kitchen was not locked, and I was hungry. I made a sandwich and took some biscuits and pudding back to the dormitory for my friends. I am sorry if I offended God, but he will understand."

"Maidy, you did wrong, and there are consequences for your actions." Sister replied.

Sister looked straight at me with a frown on her face and said, "You will not be invited back into the kitchen. You will go to the church on Saturday, and help the cleaners in the church with their cleaning duties until the end of the semester. You will get no biscuits or Christmas pudding at Christmas time. Is that clear?"

"Yes, Sister Margaret."

I left the kitchen in a hurry and bumped into my sister, Shirley, and Ellen waiting for me near the dining room.

Jeanette said, "I know what happened. Your friends told me. You were stupid, all three of you."

"Sister Margaret thinks I took the food," I said. "I told her I was the only one because I did not want to get Shirley and Ellen involved."

Shirley and Ellen thanked me, but it upset Jeanette when I told her my punishment. She left us in a huff.

I spent the next six Saturdays cleaning all the benches in the church.

Sister Matthew was in charge, and she was very bossy to

me and the other girls who were working. There was to be no conversation between us. Any questions were directed to Sister Matthew only. I was glad when the semester ended, and I no longer had to help out in the church.

Chapter 15

Jeanette Leaves Marychurch

The school year was coming to an end and the summer holidays were upon us. I had my tenth birthday in June. Everything seemed back to normal until the last day of school when my sister came knocking at the classroom door requesting me to go to Mother Superior's office. As we scurried over there I asked her what was the reason?

She said, "I don't know Maidy, a messenger came to my classroom requesting you and I to go to the office."

As we got close to the office I said, "This can't be good."

We knocked on the door and Sister told us to come in. As we entered, we saw our mother sitting on the leather armchair in the office. Jeanette ran over to Mum, but I didn't.

Sister said, "Jeanette, your mother is here to take you home today."

My sister squealed out, "Is that true Mummy?"

She nodded yes.

I said, "What about me?"

Mum answered, "Maidy, I am taking Jeanette home today, and when we get our house, I will come and fetch you. We don't have enough room in our flat for both of you."

I looked at her and said, "You can't take Jeanette from me. I don't want her to leave without me."

"Jeanette, you can't go with her," I yelled. "She can't take you away from me!"

Sister Catherine got up from her chair and came over and said, "Maidy, you will be fine, and it won't be that long before you go home too."

I stood in front of Mum and yelled, "I hate you, and Daddy hates you too." I ran out of the room leaving Jeanette in tears.

I did not go back to the classroom. Children were rushing by me as the school bell rang to dismiss them for the summer holidays. I ran behind the willow tree near the church where no one could see me. Everyone seemed so happy except me. The day students were laughing and skipping as they got on the school bus to go to their home. I wanted to scream at everybody!

I suddenly yelled, *"It's not fair. Nobody wants me! I hate my mother, and I don't like God because he doesn't listen to my prayers. My sister is leaving me and I have to stay here for how long, I don't know.".*

I walked through the garden, stopping where the stone crucifix was centered in the rose garden. I stood and looked at the cross, and then I slapped it and kicked it.

I said, "Let's face it Jesus, you want me to be unhappy. You take people I love away from me. Do you want me to be a child crowned with thorns?"

There was no answer.

I continued walking through the garden and heard my name called. I turned my head and could see my sister running towards me.

"Maidy, "I knew you would be here."

I said, "Leave me alone, and go back to our horrible mother."

"We have to go back to Mother Superior's office as she is waiting for us and has many parents waiting to see her. I will get into trouble with her and Mum if I don't come back with you, Maidy."

Under protest I walked back to the office with Jeanette.

She said, "Maidy, you will go home as soon as Mum moves into her house. I promise I will write to you and let you know what is going on."

"I will miss you so much," I said crying.

We stopped, and my sister gave me a long hug and we went into the office to see Mother Superior and Mum.

After a tearful goodbye, I left the office and Jeanette went home. My two friends, Shirley and Ellen, were waiting for me outside, and they suggested we walk to the village as this was one of our privileges that we had at ten years old.

Mum had offered me some money before she and Jeanette left Marychurch, and I took it. I showed the money to my friends, two half a crown which equaled five shillings.

I said, "We could eat some fish and chips and walk by the ocean. This cheered us all up.

Shirley said, "Maidy, I know you will miss your sister, but Ellen and I will be here for you."

"Thanks, Shirley. I don't know what I would do without you and Ellen."

"We will all have to say goodbye one day, and I am not looking forward to it happening," said Ellen.

The fish and chip shop was a two-mile walk by the ocean, and as we came closer I could smell the salty air and hear the screeching sound of the seagulls.

We stopped at the fish and chip shop, and each got a bag of thick crispy chips and a piece of breaded codfish. The man gave them to us wrapped in a newspaper and they smelled so good.

We walked down to the beach and kicked off our shoes, and socks, and sat on the warm sand watching people pass by.

We threw pebbles in the ocean and walked back to Marychurch. I was carrying a heavy heart.

The next few weeks were sad for me. I missed Jeanette, and I felt this great emptiness inside of me. I was upset with Jesus. I felt he either didn't exist, or he was fed up with me asking him to go home. Every time I walked past the music room, I looked for Jeanette. I missed seeing her playing the piano during her practice time. I stopped by the big statue of the Virgin Mary that was in the hallway leading to the dining room. I told her I was too upset to pray, because she and Jesus let me down. You sent my sister home and left me behind.

My friends had given me some space as they seemed to know what I was going through.

The worst time for me was at nighttime when I had a hard time trying to sleep. Sister Teresa continued to play her classical music at night. I would lie on my bed with my feet resting on the wall listening and crying. Sister came over to my bed one night to ask me why I was crying?

I said, "I miss my sister, and I don't know when I will see her again. I am angry with God for letting this happen once more."

Sister sat on my bed and wiped my tears with a big white cotton handkerchief.

She said, "Maidy, "I am so sorry you did not go home with Jeanette, but you can't blame God. Your mother is human and has made a human mistake."

"I hate her, Sister Teresa."

"Maidy, don't hate your mother. Pray for her."

I said, "God does not answer my prayers. Why should I pray?"

Sister replied, "Because God wants us to be happy. We will have many challenges in life, and learning from them gives us the courage and wisdom to share them with others. Try to get some sleep, Maidy. You will be with your sister soon. Just be patient and say your prayers. God loves you and will listen to you. If there is something you cannot do, ask God for his help, and this will help you to live a good life."

"Thank you, Sister Teresa. Will you play Swan Lake.?"

She smiled at me and nodded her head.

After that night I said my prayers and made peace with

God, and did my best to adjust to not seeing my sister. I broke down, and I thanked God for the nuns and my friends for daily support. During the year I asked Sister Mary who handled the post if there was a letter from Jeanette, but after so many, "No, Maidy!" replies, she would ultimately answer before I even asked.

I walked into the parking area and stood for a few minutes, taking long deep breaths. I gazed around at the beautiful gardens surrounding me. It seems like yesterday I was picking those flowers, but it was so many years ago and I keep coming back to Marychurch each year. Sometimes I wonder will I ever complete my journey?

I went into the church and sat down on the bench and watched the ladies cleaning the altar. I pulled out my rosary beads and began to pray. After I was done, I got up and lit three candles for my beloved children who have given me the gift of love and pride with being their mother.

Suzy, Donna and Jimmy.

Each one of you is different, but you all share a common denominator of compassion, love with conviction of believing in yourself and what you stand for, and caring for other people, especially immigrants.

Suzy, my first born, God gifted you with a talent in art. Through this talent, your compassion follows, and produces images that show the reality of life from joy, pain, love, sadness, and new life. You have endured many emotional struggles and upheavals in your life, especially the loss of your beloved son Christopher.

Your children's hearts are held in your hand, and your son's was taken. God has been there for you.

"Listen to God in silence and he will answer your prayers."

You are loved dearly.

I have loved being your Mum, and you certainly have given me many adventures.

Donna, my second born, God has gifted you with a talent

in teaching many subjects. Your first gift, as a special education teacher, gives you the knowledge to teach children with special needs. Many children will go out into the world with your knowledge. You are a great gardener, and I smile when I see you in my garden checking on the roses. If I need advice about cooking or fixing things I call you. You have gone through many trials and tribulations in your life and had the courage and conviction to keep moving on.

"God will be there for you, Donna, as all things are possible through God. Pray to God daily."

"No two people have been so in love as Donnie and your Mum. You are loved dearly."

Jimmy, You were my last born and blessed with many gifts in God's work through your education. Your gift is through your hands and medical knowledge which you use in teaching your students at UCSF. Through your clinics people come to you when they are physically and mentally sick, and you treat them with kindness and humility.

From a small boy you wanted to give food and money to the homeless as they were hungry and you still do. You have taken good care of your British/American Mum. Your medical knowledge allows you to spread your wings and soar high towards healing, fitness, and health. You took the longer road through obstacles and stress, but you achieved it through God's help and prayers. *"Call out God's name when you need his help and God will be there for you. Jimmy, remember to say your prayers daily with humility."*

I am so proud of all three of you, and the caring relationship you have developed with your family and friends. Caring for people in general without prejudice is why we are here on this earth. To take care of each other. *Remember family comes first! Mum loves you dearly.*

To Suzy, Donna, and Jimmy, Take care of yourself, love yourself, give yourself silence each day to help you speak to God, ask him for direction and be thankful to God for the joy in your life. You are loved dearly and will always be my two girls and one boy that gave me a gift of love and grandchildren to spoil.

I love Concord, California. The place we all spent the best years of our family life together. As I drive slowly by your schools I smile and have many happy memories throughout my lifetime. Your loving Mum XXX.

Chapter 16

The Homecoming

I was eleven and a half years old when my mother finally came to fetch me from Marychurch. I dreaded having to say goodbye to my two friends, Shirley and Ellen, and leaving Marychurch, the only home I had ever known.

I stood in front of the church and my eyes scanned the gardens. Suddenly, I felt the years tumbling back to the day before I said goodbye to my two friends. We were walking in the garden holding hands and teary eyed.

Shirley tugged my hand and said, "Maidy, I don't think I will see you again."

I answered, "You will, Shirley, because I can catch the double- decker bus to Marychurch and meet you in the village."

Ellen chimed in, "Your mother is a witch, and she will never, never, let you visit us."

I suddenly stopped walking and yelled at the top of my voice, "I will return to Marychurch. I will return. My mother is not going to stop me from seeing you."

We all sat down on the grass near the statue of the Virgin Mary. My brain was churning with deep and mixed emotions.

We held our hands together and prayed. I led the prayer, "Oh Virgin Mother please take care of us and keep our friendship together forever more."

Shirley said, "Oh Virgin Mother please watch over Maidy.

We will miss her so much." She broke down in tears. I put my arm around her and hugged her.

Ellen stood up close to the statue and said, "Virgin Mary, please watch over us until we meet again."

Suddenly, we heard a voice; it was Sister Teresa. "What are you girls doing on the wet grass?" she asked.

I said, "We were praying to the Virgin Mother. We are sad because I am going home.

Sister turned and looked straight at me and said, "Life is sad but full of adventures. You have your whole life ahead of you, Maidy, and you will meet many new friends. When you say hello, you will have to say goodbye."

I have remembered her words to this day.

When I awoke the following morning, I knew this would be the last time I would sleep in this bed.

My mother came and fetched me after breakfast. I had little time to make quick goodbyes to Reverend mother, Sister Teresa, Shirley, and Ellen. We were in tears which tore my heart in half. I wanted to stay with my friends, and I wanted to go home with my family. My mother grabbed me by the hand, and I walked through the big wooden front door of Marychurch never to return again until I was eighteen years old.

Mum and I walked to the village to catch the bus to Newton Abbot, my new home. She offered me a Mars chocolate bar, and I said, "I don't want it."

Mum said, "The bus is on time, and I don't want you crying on the bus and having everyone staring at us."

Mum and I sat in the front of the bus, and I was next to the window. I leaned my face against the cold glass, and Mum took out a book to read. To avoid any outburst, we did not speak. I kept telling myself this was a dream that I would awaken from and find out that it was a cruel joke.

I felt a deep sadness leaving Marychurch and my friends, but then there were moments when joy crept in my mind thinking of being with Jeanette and my brother Chris, and getting to know my younger sister Barbara. At long last God had answered my prayers. I was going home to live with my family, but little did I know the nightmare I would step into.

My family was living in a council house, which the government provided for needy families with low incomes. The brick house was in the middle of a row of houses all close together in a straight line in Woodland Hills, where everybody knew who lived in government housing. The bus dropped us off a quarter mile from the house. When we arrived at the house, the grass was neatly cut, and daffodils were planted on either side of the pathway. The front door was painted green with a brass letter opening and a brass doorknob. We entered the front door and went directly into the living room where the rest of the family were waiting for me.

My brother and younger sister ran up to me and both said, "Welcome home Maidy."

The first thing I noticed was my sister Jeanette, just standing there staring at me. It had been two years since I had seen her. She had gained weight and hardly spoke two words on my arrival. She had changed and was quiet and withdrawn. When she spoke it was in a whisper, and her eyes would look directly at Mum as if she needed her approval to speak.

The old Jeanette was always smiling and loved to talk about everything, but now she barely spoke two words. A week went by and it seemed like someone had wiped her smile off her face. Jeanette was moody and stayed in her room reading. I would knock on her door and she often said, "I'm busy, Maidy, come back later."

There were four bedrooms in the house. Barbara and I had to share a bedroom, and my brother and Jeanette had their own room and Mum and Andrew had the other bedroom close to mine. I didn't mind sharing the room with Barbara, but she talked about school continually, and it interfered with my reading. We could hear everything from my Mum's room, as the walls were paper-thin.

My Mother and Andrew continually bickered over money, and when they did fight Andrew would scream at the top of his voice, "If I didn't have your three swines to feed, we would have money and not be living in this bloody counsel house."

I could hear Mum crying, "Andrew, you drink every night. That is where the money is going."

Oh God, do I have to listen to this every night? How I hated him!

Andrew had a sallow face and was slim in stature and his hair was thin on top. He loved wearing a button down cardigan and had two or three in different colors. He was a compulsive smoker, and if you got close to him, you could smell the woodbine cigarettes on his clothes.

Every time he looked at me with his big beady eyes, they circled around my body. Never directly looking at me. He made my skin crawl.

When Andrew and Mum had an argument, he made snide remarks about Jeanette and me. Mum never stood up for us. She allowed him to talk down to us and never said one word in our defense. This made me feel no respect towards her. When Andrew left the house after one of their nasty quarrels, Mum was moody and displayed fits of anger by taking it out on Jeanette and me, blaming us for their fights. After one of their fights, Jeanette began to talk more to me.

Mum said, "You two swine should have stayed at Marychurch. We were a happy family until you came home."

I wanted to lash out at Mum, but Jeanette had warned me when Mum got angry, not to say one word as she would beat me and not speak to me for a week. If Mum was having one of her temper tantrums, Jeanette and I would run upstairs and both sit on the top of the stairs holding hands.

I said, "I hate living here; they don't want us!"

Jeannette whispered, "I know Maidy. We are in the way. They only want Chris and Barbara. Keep your voice low because if Barbara hears us she will tell Mum what we said to each other. How do you like sharing a room with Barbara?"

I said, "She talks continually about school and asks me questions about Marychurch."

"What questions?" Jeanette asked.

"What was it like living with a bunch of girls, and did the nuns take their hoods off at night?"

"Barbara's funny, and she laughs when Mum yells at her and gets away with it," Jeanette whispered.

I answered, "Mum only likes Barbara and Chris. We are the ones to receive the brunt of her temper, and abusive comments. We have ruined her life."

Jeanette looked at me and said, "Every time Mum and Andrew have a fight, she takes it out on us."

I took a deep breath before speaking. "When Mum talks horrible to us we have to run upstairs to our room and stay there until they call us down to eat and wash the dishes."

Jeanette laughed and said, "Maidy, you make us seem like Cinderella and Chris and Barbara are the ugly sisters.'

I said, "No, I am not Cinderella. You are. I am Jane Eyre."

Jeanette pushed me and said, "I am so glad you're here with me. I missed you so much when we were separated at Marychurch. "It was miserable coming here without you."

"I got sick to my stomach when you left without me. I cried myself to sleep for one week until Sister Teresa told me I would be going home a little later. That didn't happen for two long years."

Jeanette answered, "I cried myself to sleep whenever I thought about you, and I think it's the reason I wet the bed."

I replied, "Gosh, Jeanette, that must be awful for you. Do you still wet the bed?"

She said, "Yes, and Mum finds out when she changes the bed every two weeks. She rubs my nose in it, and I get a whipping.

"Maybe now that I am home you will stop wetting the bed."

Jeanette continued wetting her bed and being subject to Mum's abuse.

One morning I said to Jan "I heard you crying and Mum was yelling at you in your room. Was it because you wet the bed?"

Jeanette said, "Yes, and she slapped me across the face.with the wet sheet."

"I hate Mum when she gets angry."

Jeanette looked right at me and said, "Maidy, do you think I've changed?"

I responded by saying, "At first I thought you had changed, but I know now it's living with Mum. She takes her misery out on everybody, and I think she is crazy."

We both started laughing.

Jeanette and I spent many hours sitting on the stairs when we were in trouble or if we were eavesdropping on Mum and Andrew's conversations.

Sometimes when we were eavesdropping, our brother Chris joined us. He said to Jeanette and me, "I hate the way Mum talks to you girls, and her temper scares me."

I said, "Chris, her temper scares everybody."

He said, "Mum treats Barbara and me much better than you girls, but maybe it's because I am a boy and Barbara is Andrew's kid."

"Why did she bring us home?" I asked.

Chris answered, "Don't tell her I told you, but I heard Andrew and Mum talking in the kitchen about receiving a letter from Marychurch asking her when she plans to take you girls home.

Jeanette said, "What did Mum say?"

Chris lowered his voice and said, "Mum told Andrew we have to bring them home, and we will have to bring Jeanette first and Maidy after we get a council house."

I said, "It sounds like Marychurch was tiring of us."

Chris answered, "I guess so!"

I loved my brother because he was funny and would make

funny faces and talk like a duck or a cow and make us laugh. He was good at drawing animals and became an artist when he got older.

He would often tell us girls that nothing is forever and one day we could make good choices after we left home.

There was one special day a week Jeanette and I looked forward to. It was Saturdays when we were left alone in the house most of the day. This was a shopping day, and Mum would always take Barbara and Chris to the shops and leave Jeanette and I to clean the house and do the laundry and ironing.

I remember this one Saturday Jeanette was doing the ironing, and she scorched a pillowcase. I heard her crying from the laundry room and I went to see what had happened. She was standing there with the scorched pillow case in her hand and said, "Look Maidy, I burnt the pillow case and when Mum sees this, she will go crazy and beat me."

I said, "Why don't we hide it?"

Jeanette said, "We can't do that as this pillow case belongs on her bed and she only has two sets of sheets for that bed."

I said, "We will tell her we both did it."

Jeanette cried, and I put my arm around her and said, "One day we will leave home and never have to put up with her or Andrew again."

Jeanette said, "Mum scares me Maidy. I hate it when she has one of her tempers. I think one day she might kill me."

I said, "I will kill her first and that horrible drunk she is married too."

We both laughed!

I looked straight at Jeanette, and said, "How long has Andrew been drinking? He is drunk every time he goes to the pub, which is quite often."

Jeanette said, "I know, Maidy. Mum and Andrew go round and round about his drinking. He was like that when I came home from Marychurch but seems to be getting worse."

When Mum came home, she checked to see if Jeanette and I cleaned the house and then she lit the fire in the living room. When we were all gathered in the living room, I left and went upstairs and took the pillowcase out of the airing cupboard. I brought it downstairs to the living room.

I showed it to Mum and said, "When I was ironing I scorched the pillowcase."

Mum leaped off her chair and looked right at me with fire coming from her eyes and said, *"You did what?"*

I repeated, "I accidentally burnt your pillowcase."

She reached for the poker from the fireplace and struck me on the side of my face. My brother, Chris jumped up and took the poker from her. I ran out of the room into the back-yard cradling the side of my face with my hand. It was throbbing and painful, and my face was swollen. I ran to the back garden.

Mum yelled out the kitchen window, "Come into the house right now!"

I said, "No! I hate you! I want to go back to Marychurch."

Mum yelled again, "Marychurch doesn't want you, and you can stay outside all night."

It was raining, and I took shelter under a large bramble bush in the back of the garden where our two hedgehogs, named Henrietta and Harry, lived in hibernation. I sat down beside them and touched them gently. I looked up at the black clouds scrunched together in the sky and cried.

"Oh Jesus, Marychurch doesn't want me anymore. Mum doesn't want me. What am I to do? My life is miserable. Don't you and Daddy see how unhappy I am? Jesus, maybe you're not real after all; maybe you're just a fairytale, like Father Christmas."

I touched my face gently, which had swollen more on the right side, and I had streaks of blood dripping on my blouse. My lips were swollen. I felt wretched and wanted to curl up and die. But where would I go? Because I didn't believe there was a God or Jesus anymore.

Suddenly, I heard a voice. "Maidy, where are you?"

It was my brother, Chris.

I answered him, "I'm over here with the hedgehogs."

Chris came over and said, "Mum wants you to come in for tea."

I replied, "I hate her. I don't want any tea."

My brother answered, "You can't stay here all night. It's wet, and it's going to rain through the night."

"Go away, Chris. I am not going into that house until she is in bed. I will stay here with the hedgehogs because they want me."

Mum yelled out the kitchen window, "Chris come in the house. She can stay out there all night if she wants to without any tea."

Chris gave a deep sigh and went back in the house.

I lay back down on the grass, stroking the hedgehog's face with the rain lightly splashing on me. I looked up to the dark clouds and wondered if my life would ever be normal again. How I wished I could go back to Marychurch and be with my two friends, Shirley, and Ellen. Mum told me that I could not write to them as the door was closed at Marychurch, and I had to make new friends in the posh school I attended.

I must have fallen asleep. My sister Jeanette suddenly shook me awake. She was crying and said, "Oh Maidy, why did you take the blame for something I did?"

I answered, "I could not stand Mum hurting you. She has slapped your face twice this week for coming home late from school, and I could not watch her hitting you again. Your pain would be worse than mine, and I am stronger than you, Jeanette."

"I feel guilty letting you take the blame, and look at what she did to your face!"

I said, "It's okay. Please don't tell anybody. Not even Chris and Barbara. It's our secret. What time is it?"

Jeanette answered, "Almost midnight. Everybody is asleep in the house."

She stretched out her hand and I stood up; we hugged each other and went into the house. We stopped by the kitchen and I made a jam sandwich while my sister bathed my face and cleaned the wound.

Finally, we crept upstairs to our bedrooms. I got into bed, but I tossed and turned all night.

The next morning Mum acted like nothing had happened. She just ignored me.

Barbara, my younger sister, commented, "Maidy, your face has a big bruise."

Mum said, "Mind your own business Barbara, and remember, what happens in this house stays in this house. If someone asks you at school, you know nothing."

I said, "Mum, what do you want me to tell the nun when she questions me on what happened to my face?"

"You tell her you fell down the stairs and hit your face on the step."

I shook my head and went to school.

A few weeks later Mum lost her temper again! The family was sitting down to tea and Mum was pouring milk from a large jug into our cups and Jeanette said, "I don't want any milk."

But Mum poured the milk into Jeanette's cup, and Jeanette pushed the cup away from her and spilled the milk on the tablecloth. Suddenly Mum screamed at the top of her voice and said, "You stupid bloody idiot!"

We were all shocked when she broke the jug of milk on Jeanette's head. I was shaking as Jeanette slumped to the floor and passed out.

Andrew wanted to call the ambulance.

Mum screamed out loud, "I am a bloody nurse. They all know me at the hospital. I will take care of her."

Blood was gushing from a cut on the back of her head. Mum yelled at me. "Maidy, get a tea towel and give it to me."

I watched as Mum covered the wound with the tea cloth. She looked at me and said, "Put your hand on the cloth and apply some pressure."

I bent down on the floor near my sister's body with my brother. We were both shaking and crying at the same time.

I managed to hold the tea cloth on the wound with my brother's hand on top of mine. Jeanette started making whimpering sounds as I called her name.

"Jeanette, this is Maidy. Chris and I are here with you."

In the background I heard Andrew yelling at Mum, "Your temper is going to hurt someone really bad one of these days. You're bloody crazy!"

Andrew lifted Jeanette on to the couch and Mum cleaned and bandaged her wound. Jeanette had to stay home from school for two weeks. Mum told the school she had the mumps. I brought her schoolwork home each day so she could keep up with the class as she was getting ready to graduate from school.

I prayed again and told God I was sorry for telling him I didn't believe in him. I wanted him to know how much I hurt inside and why Jeanette and I were not wanted in this family?"

Days later, when I told Jeanette I had asked for God's forgiveness, Jeanette whispered, "There really is a God Maidy. It is not his fault when bad things happen. It is the fault of people who create war and bad things, but it was up to people like us to show them that there are many good things in life."

"Jeanette, I told God I don't believe he exists. Because he does not answer my prayers."

She said, "God has answered some of your prayers. We have to keep praying that Mum controls her temper."

I answered, "We will pray for her until she dies."

After Jeanette graduated from school, she left home and went into nursing training at the Royal Devon and Exeter

Hospital, and a few months after that my brother went to the Royal Navy Academy.

I was mad at them because they left me alone with the rest of the family. I was scared of Andrew, who was drinking heavily, and he and Mum were fighting all the time. It even got physical at times. I felt the need to protect Barbara and myself from both of them.

This part of my life was a journey through courage, patience, fortitude, and an inner strength to maintain my belief in God. At that time I was barely a teenager and I felt lonely, scared, and nervous each time I came home, especially after school. I never knew what mood my mother would be in, but most of the time she was miserable.

As I walked in the door her greeting was always the same. "Oh, it's you. Where is Barbara?'

Barbara got a big hug and a "Hello, darling. Did you have a good day at school?"

I went upstairs to my room and did my homework. I stayed there until Mum called me to set the table for tea, and after tea I washed the dishes and went back upstairs. I could hear Andrew, Barbara and Mum laughing together. They were happy without me around, and this was my life. In later years my Uncle Mick told me everyone in the family knew that I upset Mum because I was so much like my father, especially in my eyes and smile, and she couldn't stand to look at me, even more so after she married Andrew. She was upset with my father because he had a choice to join the service. His religion made him a conscientious objector but he did not abide with it.

I was beginning to wonder if everybody's family was as much of a mess as mine was after the war. I remember laying on my bed and hugging myself. That was my father's hug for the day.

I left the church and walked to Marychurch village. I sat down on a bench outside the gift shop and thought about Andrew, who will never know how his actions towards me affected the entirety of my life.

Chapter 17

My Spirit Weeps – The Rape

It started after we moved from the counsel house in Newton Abbot. Andrew quit his job to open a jewelry and watch repair shop in Paignton, a seaside resort, twenty miles from Newton Abbot

I was fourteen years old. My sister Jeanette was attending nursing school, where she lived at the hospital during her training. My brother was boarding at the Naval Academy in Dartmouth, South Devon.

This left my younger sister, Barbara and me at home, with Mum and Andrew. We moved into a two-bedroom townhouse in Paignton, South Devon, close to our new Catholic school. The beach was within walking distance from our new place.

My dark fearful nights began when my mother took a nursing job at the local hospital working the midnight shift. Andrew's new business was not doing well, and he was drinking rough cider every night at the local pub, coming home drunk most of the week. After school, I babysat my sister and did the house cleaning and ironing each day. Mum was in her bedroom resting and did not want to be disturbed until tea time, which she had already prepared during the day and left in a warm oven. I would set the table, and she would dish up the tea.

I had a tiny room to myself, and my sister slept in the same room as Mum and Andrew in her own bed. My bedroom started off as my sanctuary where I escaped to seek peace and serenity, disappearing into whatever book I was reading at the time.

Suddenly, it became a place of hell. Some things are too terrible to write, but if you were to peel back my skin, you would find the pain within my flesh and bones. If you were to look in my room, you would see the dark shadows of fear flickering on my walls.

My terror began on a dark wet winter night. I was lying on my bed and the rain was pelting on my window. I had grown increasingly fearful of my stepfather as lately when he brushed past me on the stairwell he would grab my breast. When I told him to stop it, he laughed in my face. There were words he whispered in a foreign accent that I dared not repeat to anybody and kept buried deep within my soul. I could not tell my mother. Her temper had gotten progressively worse, and she was more abusive than ever, especially when she was upset. What's worse, I knew she would never believe me. I knew that there was nothing I could say to win her to my side.

On this particular night I got up from my bed to check on my sister Barbara, who was sound asleep. The clock in the living room chimed twelve times. It was midnight. I heard the rattle of the key turning in the front door lock as I scurried back to my room and jumped in my bed. I lay there shaking as my stepfather climbed the creaking stairs slowly, one at a time. He stopped on the eighth stair outside my bedroom, and my heart was beating rapidly.

"Jesus," I prayed, "please don't let him come into my room. I beg you Jesus."

Suddenly I jumped as he pushed the door open and kicked it closed. I was in a fetal position on my bed. He leaned over me and ripped off my pajama top. White buttons broke off and scattered on the floor.

"Stop it!" I cried loudly, "Stop it."

He lunged on top of me, and I could hardly breathe. He ripped off my pajama bottoms and knickers. I struggled to push him away, but he was too strong for me. I could not move him off my breast as he bit on them and hurt me. I could smell the strong stench of cider and cigarettes from his breath as he tried to kiss me. I cried out loud, but to no avail.

"Shut up!" he said. "I don't want you waking Barbara."

Andrew then covered my mouth with his large clammy hand, and I lay back limp trapped on my bed as he continued to maul my body from top to bottom. I was like a limpet attached to a rock and it was painful. I thought about Marychurch and wished I was there. I felt like a sinner, someone who lost her soul to the devil. I could do nothing to stop this physical nightmare.

It was over an hour before he finally left my room, closing the door behind him, leaving my naked body draped across the bed.

As I pulled the covers over my shaking body, I could feel the dampness from the cold wet night. Tears flooded my eyes and my mouth was sore. I banged my head on the pillow and then started punching it.

"Oh God, what just happened?" I thought. "Where were you? I've been attacked by the devil."

I wanted to get up and go to the bathroom and scrub my whole body clean, but I was too scared to leave my room for fear he would come back. My breasts were so sore and he had left bruises between my legs. I felt sick within my very soul and dirty inside and out.

"Jesus, where were you?" I whispered. "I needed you!"

I lay awake for hours staring at the white ceiling in a daze wondering what to do. I thought of my two friends Shirley and Ellen at Marychurch. Mum had forbidden me to contact them after I left the orphanage, and I missed them. I knew deep inside I could talk to them about my situation. But it has been two years since we last spoke to each other. I thought they were probably upset with me as I had not written to them. I had tried a couple of times, but when Mum found out she screamed at me.

"Maidy, I will beat the hell out of you if I find out you have anything to do with bloody Marychurch. I hate that place!"

From that moment, I knew I could never tell her anything.

I didn't want to tell my sister, Jeanette. I was worried that she might quit college if she were to find out. I definitely could not say anything to my brother, especially about sex.

My eyes brimmed with tears as I pulled out my rosary and started to pray to the Virgin mother.

"Oh, Mother of Jesus please ask him to stop Andrew from hurting me," I said out loud.

Finally, I fell asleep.

The next day I got up and dressed in my school uniform and went downstairs. Andrew was sitting in the kitchen with Barbara and they were both laughing together. He asked me if I wanted cereal, and I said,

"No, I'm not hungry. I'm leaving for school."

I went back upstairs to get my school bag, and Andrew followed me. He pushed me against the door and grabbed my breast. I yelled out Barbara's name, and she came running upstairs as he went back down.

"Are you ready for school Barbara?" I asked.

"Yes," she said.

On the way to school I asked Barbara, "Did you hear any noise last night?"

She said, "No, why did something happen?"

I said, "Nothing happened. It was pouring rain and the wind was howling, and I wondered if it woke you up."

"No, I slept all night. Once I fall asleep, I hear nothing," she said.

We did not mention it again. This incident rented space in my brain all day. I looked around the classroom and there was no one I could speak to, not even Sister Anne, the teacher. No one would believe me.

Andrew came back the following night and many nights to come. I recorded each night Andrew came to my room as a dark night. These events happened twice a week and sometimes three times. I started thinking about joining my father in Heaven. Maybe I could run in front of the bus or a car, or I could walk in the ocean until I drowned. I had so many crazy thoughts in my head planning to get away from Andrew.

Mum was off two nights a week and those nights were inscribed in my heart as my white nights. Andrew would not come into my room when Mum was home. When Mum worked, these were my black nights; stored with hidden secrets I could speak to no one.

The hospital where Mum worked was a ten minute walk through the village and up a short hill. In the winter months Mum wanted me to go with her to work at 10:00 P.M. to carry her bag with her knitting, books, and snacks.

Barbara was sleeping at that time.

One night I wanted to say something to Mum about Andrew, but I couldn't as we were not close. We very rarely talked as we walked to her job. I knew she knew when we reached the hospital. She took the bag from me and said, "Run home to Barbara."

I did run through the village as I was scared, especially when I passed the pubs and the fish and chips shop. I was usually home at ten-thirty.

I remember being obsessed with the stairs knowing every creek and step taken by Andrew. They were my strongest warnings to signal me whether it would be the dark night, or I had a white night of freedom.

On Saturdays I had to clean our townhouse while Mum and Barbara were out shopping. Andrew was at work so I had the place to myself. I remember this one Saturday being one of the blackest days of my life.

I was dusting in the living room where there was a small wooden table in the corner. This was where Andrew repaired watches at home. When I was dusting the table I saw this beautiful gold watch, and I tried it on. It fitted me perfectly. I was wearing my long sleeve school cardigan, which covered the watch. I continued cleaning and forgot all about the watch.

When Mum came home, she was fixing the tea, and she called out my name. I went into the kitchen and she said, "Maidy, set the table for tea as your father will be home any minute."

I hated her when she called that man my father, but I answered, "Mum, should I put out soup spoons?"

"No!" she said.

Before I finished setting the table for tea, Andrew walked in the kitchen and gave me a frozen stare.

We all sat down for tea and Barbara said, "Maidy, please pass me the jam."

As I reached across the table to pass her the jam, she said, "I like your watch."

All hell broke loose.

Mum got up and grabbed the watch away from me screaming, "Where did you get that watch from?"

Andrew looked at the watch and said, "She took it off my table, and it belongs to one of my customers."

I immediately ran upstairs with them both chasing after me to my room. Mum shoved me on the bed and ordered Andrew to give me a beating.

She stood there with Barbara crying from the doorway, "Don't hurt her! Don't hurt her!"

Mum yelled to Barbara, "Go downstairs, or I will beat you too."

Andrew beat the hell out of me with his fists while my mother stood and watched, until she finally yelled, "Stop it Andrew. That's enough!"

They both left my room. I could hardly stand up as my

body was stiff and sore. I had welts all over my body, and he gave me a black eye which had swelled to a point where I could not see out of it.

I limped over to the window and looked up at the sky. I called Daddy's name. "Daddy, I need your help," I said. "I have prayed to Jesus, but I don't think he can hear me."

"Daddy, tell Jesus I did not mean to steal the watch, I was just going to borrow it, as it was so shiny and pretty."

I heard the clock chime at 7:00PM. After two and a half hours Mum had come back to my bedroom holding a wet cloth and told me to lie down and put the wet towel over my eye.

"How could you let that man beat me?" I asked.

"You're a stupid idiot, and you brought this on yourself," she said. Tomorrow you stay home from school."

"Why?" I asked, "Because you don't want the nuns to know I got beaten?"

"You will stay up in this room, and I will bring your meals," she replied.

I stayed in my room, and Andrew did not come near me during that time. I had eight white nights and my eyes and welts got better, and I read three books on Sue Barton, about a student nurse going through her nursing training. Mum picked them up from the local library for me.

I was feeling a taste of freedom. Mum had been calm and even nice to me, and Barbara checked in on me and let me know daily how my eye was looking.

I started back to school and saw Andrew that morning. He completely ignored me, which gave me a deep satisfaction thinking that maybe he would stay away from me now. But that was wishful thinking on my part.

For the next three nights, Andrew stumbled up the stairs drunk and stopped on the eighth stair while I held my breath, and then he went into his room and slammed the door shut. I decided after the beating he gave me he would not bother me anymore.

On the fourth night, I was feeling my old self and heard Andrew's key in the lock at 11:30 P.M. and I turned my light off and ignored him stumbling up the stairs.

Suddenly, he burst into my room and kicked the door shut.

He said, "I've missed you and I want you. Take that nightdress off!"

I said, "No! "Do this with Mum! Not me!"

Andrew answered, "Your mother is a cold bitch, and she is crazy."

As he started ripping off my nightgown I said, "Please Andrew, don't do this to me!"

He covered my mouth with his lips and I wanted to throw up with the smell of the rough cider. He hurt my breasts by pinching them with his rough hands. I pushed him off the bed. He pulled my hair and threw me back on the bed. He buried his face in my breasts while his hands wandered over my body.

"I hate you!" I yelled.

Finally he got up and left the room.

"God, this has to end now!" I said.

I heard his bedroom door slam, and I got up and got dressed in my school uniform. I put my raincoat on as it was raining outside.

I crept downstairs and went into the kitchen and washed my face with the dishcloth. The clock chimed one o'clock. I knew that this had to end or I would commit suicide. I could not take it anymore. I looked in the mirror in the hallway, and I noticed I had bite marks on my neck and body and blood coming from my lip where Andrew bit it.

I walked out the front door down onto the main street which was deserted. As I passed the Catholic Church, I saw a light in the priest's house. I went to the front door and reached up to the brass door knocker and banged it hard.

Father O'Neil answered the door, and it shocked him to see me standing there. He said, "Maidy, what are you doing here at this time of the night? Is something wrong with your mother?"

I said, "Father, I don't know where to go. I need to speak to you."

He said, "Come in, my child."

I followed father into the living room and stood there and opened my raincoat and showed him the bite marks on my neck and legs.

"Who did this to you Maidy?" he asked.

"My stepfather, Andrew," I replied. "He raped me, father!"

Father looked right at me with a dismayed look on his face and said, "Where is your Mother? Does she know about this?"

"She is working the midnight shift at the hospital," I answered, "and no, I have not told her because she might beat me and not believe me."

Father said, "I believe you Maidy, and you are not going back home tonight. I am taking you over to the convent where you go to school and I will speak to Mother Superior and ask her to take you as a boarder."

It was the early hours of the morning and Father took me to the convent riding his bike with me sitting on the handlebars, and the rain was spitting down on us, but for the first time I felt freedom. I prayed to God, and said, "Thank you."

As we got close to the convent Father said, "How long has your step father been bothering you?"

"Almost two years," I said.

He said, "May the Blessed Virgin mother watch over you from this day forth."

We arrived at the convent at 2:30AM. Father rang the doorbell and knocked on the door. Sister Mary answered the door and the look on her face was one of complete shock when she saw Father and I standing there.

"Sister," father said, "we have an emergency with Maidy and her family. We need your help."

Sister ushered us both into the living room and left the room with the priest. She looked back at me and said, "Maidy, you are safe here, and I will be back to fetch you soon."

I sat in the nuns' living room for almost half an hour, and I heard Sister Mary say goodnight to Father O'Reilly. Sister came back to the living room and told me to come with her.

As I followed her she said, "Maidy, you will sleep in the nuns' quarters tonight. I will contact the Air Ministry in the morning to request that you become a full-time boarder at this convent until you graduate from school."

"Thank you Sister," I replied.

Sister Mary woke me up the following morning to tell me my mother was in her office very upset and would like to see me.

"No Sister," I said. "I hate her."

"Maidy, get dressed and I will not leave your side as long as she is there," replied Sister Mary.

As we entered the room Mum got up from her chair and walked towards me and said, "Maidy, tell Sister that it is not true about Andrew touching you."

I stayed close to Sister Mary and said, "I hate you for what you have put me through since coming home from Marychurch. You are a bully, and Andrew is a bully, and yes, he raped me and kept touching me while you were at work. It has been almost two years."

"You're a liar, Maidy," she said. "Tell Sister it did not happen."

Sister lifted my skirt and opened my blouse and said to my mother, "What are these marks on this girl? Don't tell me this did not happen. You should be ashamed of yourself."

Mum looked at me and said, "You and I are through." She walked out of the convent.

Sister Mary said, "She knows what she has done to you. You will stay with us at the convent."

The Air Ministry granted my boarding fees at the convent, and for the next three years I was at peace with the nuns. I spent my school holidays with them, as my mother did not want me home again, which was fine with me.

My sister Jeanette visited me at the convent not long after

I started living there and she broke some very difficult news to me.

"Maidy, Andrew is dead," she told me.

"Dead?" I replied. "How? When? I don't understand."

"Mum threatened to turn him over to the police for what he had done," Jeanette said. "And he took his life."

I was traumatized by this news. I started banging my head against the wall. I looked at my sister, and said, "I killed him."

She put her arms around me and said, "No Maidy, he killed himself. That was his choice and it was because Mum wanted a divorce for humiliating her and because he raped you."

Mum never came over to the convent to visit me. She believed I wrecked her marriage, and there was no redemption. I hated her.

My sister and brother visited me often. My sister told me when she visited Mum she was always with Aunt Ruby, and they both told her I had ruined Mum's life, and she wished I had stayed at Marychurch.

Jeanette said, "Mum is angry most of the time, complaining about you, and everybody who upsets her."

"She has been like that since I got to know her," I said, "and I'm glad I am not around to hear her."

Within three years Mum got married again.

I was not invited to their wedding. My brother told me he was a nice guy and they seemed happy together. I was happy boarding at the convent and the sisters were endearing, teaching me that God gives us two important gifts when we come into this world.

One is the gift of life to live and learn.

The second is the gift of kindness, to love thy neighbor as well as thyself.

After I graduated from school, I joined the Royal Air Force. I entered their Nursing program in Swindon, which is eighty-two miles from London.

Chapter 18

Off to Boot Camp

I chose to serve in the Royal Air Force because it had been my father's choice, and the air force had paid for my private school education in my teenage years at The Convent of the Holy Ghost boarding school in Paignton, Devon, where mostly rich girls went to school. Me, a poor girl living in a counsel house, trying to fit in using my intellect. My uniform was always too big as it belonged to my sister Jan who was much taller than me. The abuse I received from my classmates was made worse by my mother who curled my hair with pipe cleaners, which had the effect of frizzing my hair. With my darker skin, the kids in my class called me a Gollywog or a half-cast.

It was a rainy day when I left home to join the Royal Air force. There were dark gray clouds hovering in the sky. I felt cold and sick inside my stomach, but saying goodbye to Mum was easy. There were no hugs and no tears. I let out a sigh of relief as I boarded the train. It took courage to finally leave. I had graduated from school and had nowhere to go. Deep down inside I felt scared for the unknown. I was proud of myself knowing it was my choice to leave Devon and join the RAF.

I chose nursing as a career because I believed the pain I had lived through would make me a more compassionate care provider. I dreamed of this moment many times, and the day had finally come. My sister Jeanette was finishing her nursing training at the Royal Devon and Exeter Hospital, and I was beginning mine. Jeanette had flourished since leaving home for nursing school. Not only had she regained her self-confidence, but she had also made new friends. She was born to be a nurse and loved looking after her patients in the hospital. Jeanette was happy to be away from home and having her independence.

I boarded the train to Wilmslow, Manchester, the location of the RAF boot camp with only two shillings in my pocket. My mother had given me the money, reminding me when I got paid, I was to give it back to her. This money was to be used on my trip, which was a solid nine-hour ride. My destination was the RAF. Wilmslow, the Boot training camp in Manchester.

During the train ride I was hungry. I had eaten nothing for breakfast. I spent two shillings on a pasty, potato crisps, biscuits, and a mug of tea. According to my mother, someone would pick me up at the station in Wilmslow and take me to the base. I arrived at Winslow station at 7:30 P.M., and there was nobody outside to take me to the base. I asked the porter at the station if a bus comes by to take recruits to the Air Force base.

He said, "No, you catch the double-decker bus, which will drop you by the base. The bus comes by every hour until 1:00AM. and the base is three miles on the country road." I had no money left for the bus fare and a heavy box suitcase to carry. I began to walk up the dirt road dragging my suitcase behind me. It was out in the country and the lights from the sheep's eyes guided me as I walked past them in the darkness on a bitter cold dark night in October. I knew the cows were close from the smell of their dung.

After walking a mile, I stopped and rested near a wooden gate leading to a field which smelt of Brussels sprouts. I thought about the two shillings Mum gave me, and how I hated her for not giving me enough money, and the torment she had put me through after coming home from Marychurch. I always felt like an intruder in my home.

I walked past a dairy farm, and wished I could drink the milk sitting there ready for delivery. I stopped to rest after my second mile and plopped down on the damp grass with my boxed suitcase. The silence of the night was scary and I was alone. Occasionally you heard the cows and sheep nearby, which was a comfort to my soul. I got up and brushed the grass off my skirt. I felt dirty and hungry. I needed a hot bath before going to bed. I looked at my watch and it was almost midnight. As I walked my last mile I felt blisters forming on both heels.

Suddenly, in the distance I could see many buildings lit up, and a sign on the side of the road, RAF Wilmslow. Finally, I arrived at the base and one of the guards walked in my direction to meet me.

"Your late young lady," he said.

"I know, and I look messy," I said, "and I need a bath and some food."

"My name is Greg," he said. "You are a knockout. Do you have a boyfriend?"

"Stop flirting with me and help me to my quarters," I said in an aggravated tone. "Here are my documents."

After scanning my information with his eyes, he looked at me and said, "June Suzette Houghton. Eighteen years, from Devon".

"Greg, I am tired," I said.

He took me to the new arrivals barracks where I had been assigned. Greg walked in with my suitcase and I followed. We were met by a bunch of screaming girls laying on their beds.

They started yelling, "Get out, get out".

He said, "It's okay girls, just helping a pretty girl." Greg waved at me and said, "Good Luck."

There were twenty beds set up like a dormitory in a long wooden hut. I had my name in big letters printed on a card which was perched in the middle on bed nineteen near the door. The girls were friendly and welcomed me.

The girl sitting on the bed next to mine said, "I'm Lizzy. "What took you so long to get here?"

"I'm June, and I came from Devon on a train to Manchester, which took nine hours. Where can I get something to eat?"

She laughed and said, "Come with me."

I followed her to the front of the hut and there was a room on the corner which was a large kitchen. The table was laden with sausage rolls, eggs, ham, and cucumber sandwiches. I saw two sponge cakes half eaten.

Lizzie said, "This food was brought over from the base mess hall for the new arrivals. It's been sitting here all day".

Lizzy and I both packed a plate with food and giggled at the large amount we had taken. As we were leaving more girls were coming into the kitchen. After I ate my supper, Jan, the girl who slept on the other side of me, showed me where the bathrooms were. I soaked in the tub thinking of my next new ventures in life. It was 2:30AM when I went into my hut, and the lights were out. I crawled into my bed and thanked God for my new life serving in the WRAF.

This was my home where I spent six weeks in rugged training. I was very thankful that I had been good at sports in school. My drill sergeant was tough, but nice to me as I was athletic which helped me get through those grueling six weeks.

I was sorry when the training was complete, but enjoyed the circle of friends I had made at the base and the local pub. We seemed to celebrate something every night, but everyone was happy and perhaps a little drunk. The pub was constantly thick with smoke from cigarettes, and like everyone else, I smoked. I started to smoke when I was fifteen in high school, bumming cigarettes from anyone, and picking up stubs from around the school area where the workmen worked, as I could not afford to buy them. Since joining the WRAF, I chain smoked in the pubs; sometimes I would puff on a pipe full of tobacco.

I got paid twice a month. Mum had filled out a form through the RAF to allocate half of my money to her. She told the pay officer that she was saving it for me through the local post office, but she lied. She told me she needed the money for herself. I managed to save two shillings each month through the post office. I ate all my meals on base and if I went to a pub, I drank shandies as they were the cheapest drink. It was a mix of beer and lemonade. Sometimes a bloke would buy me a drink.

I remember one night at the pub when I was attending a party with my girlfriends when I had too much to drink. Suddenly, I was doubled over with sharp pains in my tummy. My friends thought I was drunk until I fainted on the floor.

I remembered waking up at the base hospital with a medical officer hovering over me. He was trying to locate my pain. After a thorough examination he told me I had to have surgery as I needed my appendix removed, but he couldn't do the surgery until some liquor had evaporated.

Early the next day I had the surgery. I was feeling embarrassed at my condition upon entering the base hospital, but no one said anything regarding me being drunk on admittance. On my discharge the medical officer said to me, "Watch your alcohol drinking, especially if you plan to enter nursing school. We don't need drunk nurses working at the base hospital." I nodded my head and saluted him.

The following week I received my orders to transfer to Wharton Medical Hospital, the RAF base in Swindon, eighty-two miles outside London. This was also the medical training base hospital where I would spend my next three years in nursing school. I was sad when I said goodbye to all my friends at Wilmslow, but I felt a new sense of strength, which I had gained during serving my time there.

I remember my sister saying, "When you say hello, you say goodbye. When you say goodbye, you say hello to a new friend." I have spent most of my life saying hello and goodbye. The first day at my new base in London, I met three girls during our orientation. They turned out to be my dearest friends during nursing school, and my bridesmaids when I got married. We shared the same hut, with our bunks next door to each other for the duration of my time. The hut was the same as Wilmslow, with twenty bunks. We had a kitchen and bathrooms which were located to the side of the building.

We had a loudspeaker in our hut which piped in music from the base and any announcements. On Sundays there was one hour of music requested by the base personnel. You would know if a guy was interested in you if they would request a song for you, and this was the same with the girls if they were interested in a guy. I never followed up on my request. My friends were Jan, Daphne and Brenda; they were all streetwise. Jan was a little tougher, but they taught me a few things about life from their experiences. I can remember the first night in the dorm we talked all night about our goals and dreams for the future. They talked about marriage and men. I listened to them.

They were astonished that a convent-boarding schoolgirl joined the service. They nicknamed me Sister June because I would say my rosary at night, and I wore a long flannel nightgown to bed. When they discussed men, I would clam up trying to change the subject. After the ordeal of my childhood, I did not want a man. My friends and I would go out to the various pubs in town and drink and party. We all loved to dance. When Elvis Presley came on the radio singing "All shook up," we danced on our beds in our dorm and sang together. This would lead to shrieking with laughter and throwing pillows at each other. I shared their makeup and clothes. I owned nothing but a change of clothes and ten books, which I brought with me. We practically did everything together and bonded as sisters.

Our base was next door to an American base, and we were all very skeptical about the "Yanks." There were rumors they had left many British women pregnant from World War II, and this was a big turnoff for me. Also, the British men on our base called nurses who dated Americans, "Yankee Bashers." Little did I know that I would become one of them.

Burderop Park American base, held dances in their club on Saturday nights, and the buzz at the hospital was that their dances had wild music and you could dance until 2:00 A.M. This piqued my interest as I loved to dance, especially rock-and-roll. I remember going with a group of nurses to the American club on a Saturday night. I danced until the early hours of the morning. The Americans would hold you very close to them when they danced a slow dance, which made me feel a little uncomfortable. I was attracted to the American accent and saw the language differences.

My friends and I made the club our Saturday night entertainment, but I avoided getting involved with the American men. After my traumatic childhood I was scared to death of men and only wanted them as friends. I remember the nightly conversations we had in the nurses' dorm, regarding the Americans being aggressive in their pursuit of sex. My friend Jan joked with me saying, "Maidy likes to dance but when men come to ask her to slow dance, she runs to the ladies' room."

Everybody in the dorm laughed except me. In the dark I lay awake in a cold sweat, feeling the dampness on my pillow, wondering how I would overcome the fear of being touched by a man. The thought of sex with a man nauseated me. I knew men were attracted to me, and eventually I would meet this obstacle head on. I kept my secret from my friends. When they questioned me about my virginity. I used my Catholicism as my defense, telling them it was a sin to have sex unless you were married.

I spent as much time as possible either studying anatomy and physiology or reading my classics or Sue Barton nurse books. I was given the nickname "Flash" by my friends as I was the first student to answer a question in class, and I was fast giving injections, when I worked in the TB ward.

I loved sports, especially field hockey. I had the honor of playing the goalkeeper for the medical team, and after each game I was covered in bruises even though I wore my protective pads. After a game I would soak in the bathtub to heal my wounds and try to conceal the bruises with makeup before going to the American club, but my dance partners noticed the bruises and would inevitably ask me if someone had beaten me up. It immediately took me back to my childhood and realized the wounds deep down were more painful than the ones from the hockey games. I told the Americans I played hockey for the Air Force and was the goalkeeper, which impressed them more than my British accent.

I can remember pinching myself at night after coming home from the dances with my friends to assure me this was not a dream. For the first time in my life I was enjoying myself, and I could laugh and giggle and let my hair down and have fun. When I got back to the base and tumbled into my bed. I would lie awake for hours wondering how long this fun would last. Some nights I would wake up in a cold sweat and have these strange thoughts of dying. These thoughts wouldn't go away. I was developing obsessive compulsive disorder or OCD but did not know it at the time.

The struggle to enjoy life when happiness prevailed was so overwhelming that I forced myself not to enjoy my life for fear it would be swept away from me. These thoughts were consistent. This was my secret, which I could not tell anybody.

Some say, "The eyes are the windows to the soul."

When I joined the Air Force I saw my first glimmer of a rainbow with many bright colors for my future, which almost blinded my eyes. I felt happy to feel needed by people who became my friends. My father's life was taken from the Air Force because of war, but the Air Force had given me back my life. I will be forever grateful to them and to God. I remember many fond memories.

Chapter 19

Learning to Love and Understand Me

During my nursing program I met a charming, caring, American serviceman named Bill Gatewood who was from Portsmouth, Virginia. I met Bill on the American Base in the NCO. club. I was dancing a slow dance with another American serviceman when Bill kept bumping into me on the dance floor. All I could remember was his beautiful smile and Southern accent. I had seen him working in the administrative office as the secretary to the base captain. I had gone out on a few dates with the captain, and Bill wasted no time in telling me the captain was married and had a wife with three children back home in the States. Bill was also a regular fixture at the NCO club, where he worked as a part-time waiter.

After my dance ended, I went to the ladies' room and he followed me.

"I am going to follow you in there unless you agree to a date with me," he said.

I laughed out loud. "Fine. Fine, I'll go out with you," I replied.

Many dates followed after the first one. We fell in love. I told him everything about my childhood and the many struggles I had faced, and he was a constant source of strength and comfort to me. After a whirlwind courtship, Bill and I got married at the same club where we met. Two hundred military personnel attended the wedding. Because Bill worked at the club, all the men who worked with him volunteered to be servers at our wedding reception.

The captain of the base supplied the champagne. We were married October 17, 1960, when autumn leaves were dropping all around us. I wore a beautiful white lace dress dripping with pearls running down the front of my dress. It was a drizzling rainy wet day. I remember wearing white satin shoes, and as I entered the Catholic Church to get married, I stepped into a huge puddle.

The muddy water splashed my new shoes and my wedding dress. I started to cry when suddenly, I heard the organ playing and saw all my friends and family in the church. The sight of them filled me with happiness. I told myself this is your day, and nobody can take it away from you. This was such a special day because it filled me with many dreams for the future, and I yearned to have a family to love and be loved.

Walking down the aisle accompanied by my stepfather Owen, I could see the faces turned towards me, and standing in front of the altar was Bill and his best man Jim Featherlin, both smartly dressed in their Air Force uniforms. I felt like I was walking on clouds, and I had to pinch myself to reassure me that this was not a dream. I gazed at the altar and thanked God for giving me this special day.

Suddenly, I felt anxiety and fear that this could not be happening. Only sadness should be in my life, and if I face happiness, someone will snatch it from me. And then, I heard my father's voice saying,

"Maidy, this is your wedding day, and you deserve to be loved and given a happy future."

But he was not here to see me on my special day. Those uneasy feelings emerged to take a rented space in my brain and in my life. I have learned to live with these obsessive-compulsive thoughts. They have become part of my daily habits. These inner thoughts tried to master my mind and demand more time than I cared to give. They flashed back and forth trying to convince me I was not worthy to receive love from anybody. At night I would pray feverishly to God to help relieve my mind, at short periods my mind was at peace, but then something would trigger these obsessive thoughts back into my brain again.

I continued to walk up the aisle, where Owen gently took my arm and put it into Bill's. He lifted my veil and my eyes were bright with hope. The base chaplain had us recite our vows and we were married. Bill kissed me, and our new life began.

The cooks on Bill's base who catered the wedding reception made a huge wedding cake, which everybody enjoyed. My family attended the wedding and was overwhelmed with all the military personnel and the attention I was getting.

At the reception I spotted my Auntie Ruby going back and forward to the buffet table filling her purse with turkey. When the waiter asked her what she was doing, she told him she wanted to take meat home for her cat. My Uncle told me later that he was going to eat the turkey for lunch for the rest of the month of October. Bill laughed.

Bill thought I had a very unusual family and found them all very interesting, especially my mother. Bill was always very respectful to my family, and my family loved and welcomed Bill. Through Bill, I maintained a much better relationship with my mother, but I never forgave her for the mental and physical abuse she inflicted upon me as a child.

Our wedding gifts were placed on the stage in the club at the USAF base. I was in awe; I had never seen so many gifts, and they were all for Bill and me. I had never received more than two presents, and that was for my birthday and at Christmas time. When Bill and I had to get up on the stage to open them, I was lost for words.

I looked out into the audience and heard Mum yelling out about the clock she gave us for our wedding gift. She told me to open it first. I looked at her and thought of the china clock she had given to us. I had seen it in the house when she was married to Andrew. This clock reminded me of the few wasted years with her verbal abuse and how she had missed my childhood. I don't know why my mother gave me her clock for our wedding gift. When it was mailed to the States to our new home in Virginia, the clock arrived in 100 pieces. I told Bill it was an omen and he put the pieces in the trash.

I looked up at Bill and thanked God for making our paths meet. Our fate had been sealed from the moment we first met. With this American alongside me I walked with confidence. He would take me to America, a land of opportunity. With him I saw a whole New World and hoped for the future. I would live in a place where I could be free at long last.

I was sad to say goodbye to my three special friends and my beloved England, but I had heard many wonderful things about America from my sister. Jeanette had already moved to America. She had gone to the States as an exchange graduate registered nurse and had settled in Chicago. She worked at The Little Company of Mary Hospital and loved her job and the American people. When she heard the news about Bill and me, she cried with joy.

She said, "This was the hand of God joining us together again."

We had missed each other more than we cared to admit. When she went to America, I told her I would join her one day soon, but never in my wildest dreams did I think that I would meet an American and move to the United States. Jeanette had met someone special in Chicago, and they were planning on getting married in a few months. We both felt that luck had finally found us.

Bill's and my wedding party continued with the band music until the wee hours of the morning. Bill and I escaped at 10: 00 PM and went to our new rented flat in the town of Swindon. Bill was good to my family, and I will be forever grateful.

Shortly after we married, I was honorably discharged from the RAF, and Bill and I moved to Orlando, Florida where we spent the first couple years of our marriage. Bill was stationed at the USAF base, and I worked at the Orange Memorial hospital in the emergency room as a nurse. We rented a mobile home from a farmer close to the base, and it was surrounded by oranges and grapefruit groves. I never saw an orange until I was sixteen years old. It was at the open market in London and too expensive for me to buy. Here they were dropping at my back door, and I was eating them daily for free.

I remember one night Bill was at the base and we had a bad rainstorm, which scared me. Our tin roof was making a dreadful noise as if it was being hit by raining tennis balls. I peeped outside the back door, and I was attacked by oranges and grapefruit. The trees were swaying back and forth.

In 1962 we moved after Bill was honorably discharged from the military. We moved to Richmond, Virginia, where I had two beautiful daughters, Suzy, and Donna.

America was the beginning of a new life with many adventures. I was seeing new places, meeting Bill's family and making friends. American culture was different from the British world I grew up in. We were more conservative in our way of life. Americans were open minded and friendly. People hugged each other every time they met. I felt uncomfortable when Bill's family tried to hug me. I never saw any of my relatives hug each other. Our lives were full of secrets kept in the pandora's box.

In America there was freedom of speech, where women discussed their private life, and asked many questions about yours when they first met you. In England you were taught never to discuss your personal life or your marriage. But the memories of my childhood constantly flicked back and forth, taking up space in my brain causing much mental anguish and sickness. Bill was very supportive and did not question me. He knew I had grown up in an orphanage and understood the relationship I had with my mother.

I fell in love with America and found my heart was torn between both countries. But I had to go back home. My night sweats had turned into bad dreams. Hearing sirens blaring defiantly over a loud roar of German planes, dropping bombs all around me. I was running to the nuns at Marychurch but fell into a ditch with crying children. These nightmares sucked out so much energy from my body, leaving me exhausted carrying an additional burden, by keeping secret from my family in America. I also continued to obsess about my past. I carried so much blame for Andrew's death. When my two daughters were born, I was possessed with thoughts of them being taken from me. I did not share these thoughts with Bill. I was worried what he would think.

After living in Virginia for five years, we moved to California and settled in the Bay Area. We bought a modest home in Concord and raised our two daughters before our son, James, came along. I continued to work as a nurse and Bill entered the candy business, where he worked as a broker for many years.

Bill and I divorced after fifteen years of marriage, which most of the time was good. Bill was a decent man and had worked hard all his life. I will always be grateful to Bill for taking me away from a dysfunctional home and bringing me to America. I have often thought that if I had not married Bill, I would have stayed in England, and perhaps my life would be very different from what it is today. We had three wonderful children whom we loved dearly and have shared this common bond until Bill died, November 30, 2018.

My purpose

We come to this earth with a purpose
Our past experiences revealed
Through the guidance of the soul
       Which unfolds our wisdom within
To focus on human endeavor
And truly engage the knowledge, on why are we here?
The body becomes receptive to pain
Prejudice, tolerance, and love
It assimilates within consciousness
       Education is important
To assist in service towards humanity
       Knowing the most important concept
To love, to forgive, and treat each other as equals
It is necessary to align our body and soul
       With reflection and awareness
That our personality develops, evolving
       Through growth and perception of yourself
We invoke compassion, love, and mercy, to people around us
Through understanding our purpose in life
       To know why I am here
              Maidy, June Houghton

Chapter 20

Silence Is Refreshment for the Soul

I can remember that awful day in April 1976 when my brother-in-law, Rusty, called me in California. I was standing in the kitchen making lunch for the family, when Bill handed me the phone, and I saw the expression on his face. I knew something had happened to my sister, who was in The Little Company of Mary hospital in Chicago. I started to shake as I grabbed the phone from Bill. I felt a clammy hand take hold of me as Rusty, her husband, spoke the terrible news that would change my life from that day forward.

My sister was in surgery to remove a polyp from her colon. The surgeons discovered a metastasized tumor and suspected stage four cancer. I was heartbroken by the news, especially after I had talked to her doctor. I wished my I didn't have a nurse's knowledge at that moment, because I didn't want to know the consequences of my sister's disease.

Thank God, Bill was with me when I got the terrible call as I was a total mess. Immediately, he called the airlines to book a flight for me to go to Chicago. This was one of many during the year of 1976. I remember saying goodbye to my children and Bill at San Francisco International Airport. The children were crying, and Bill was worried about my mental condition as my OCD was acting up. I was so angry with God. I couldn't understand why he wanted to take my sister from her two little boys and me. I can remember running outside to the backyard and screaming out loud.

"God, how can you do this to me? You have taken my father, and I know you want my sister. I hate you God! I hate you!"

In the summertime, I asked Jeanette's husband, Rusty, to send my sister and my nephews to stay with me for six weeks. Those six weeks were so painful as I watched my sister suffer mentally and physically from her disease. Her body was frail, and she was unable to walk without one of us physically supporting her.

I remember sitting on the couch with her and feeling her cold feet pressed against my knees. I would rub her feet and put my thick ski socks on them. Jeanette would just lie there and smile at me. I remember giving her a record of Gladys Knight and the Pips singing, "You are the Best Thing that Ever Happened to Me." She played this record over and over again on her small record player.

"Don't you ever forget that you were the best sister that God could have given to me," she said.

We both cried, because deep down we knew we were soon going to have to say goodbye to each other. We treasured the moments when the children were to bed. We would lie on the soft brown couch in the family room one at each end. We talked about the orphanage, the family, and our kids.

Jeanette said, "I never want our children to feel unloved and rejected as we had felt with our mother."

"We were scared of Mum," I replied. "She had a terrible temper that ignited at the drop of a hat. When we came home from the orphanage we were in our teens, and we were horrified at Mum's temper tantrums and terrified of her and my stepfather's drinking."

I reassured Jeanette that we were good mothers, and we had done the best job we knew how in raising our children. Furthermore, our children would forever know the meaning of a mother's love and would respect us. Jeanette often fell asleep during our conversations, and I would lay with her with my thoughts turning to God, hoping he would cure her cancer. After seeing how weak she was when she came to visit me, I knew deep inside her disease was fatal.

Chapter 21

Looking for a Miracle

We prayed to St Jude for a miracle, but time was running out. Jeanette would suddenly wake up from her nap and continue our last discussion on the kids.

"They will never know the meaning of rejection from us," she said. "I don't want my sons talking about me not being a caring mother, I love them with all my heart and soul."

"Maidy, when we were in the orphanage, I tried to take care of you like a mother, and a sister, but you would get very angry when we took those bus trips to visit Mum," Jeanette said.

"Because we were in the way," I said. "We would arrive at Mum's place at lunchtime and could only stay long enough to eat lunch and return home. I remember watching Mum fixing us spaghetti on toast, and you would take forever to eat it. I knew you wanted to stay as long as possible. But I wanted to get back on the bus and return to Marychurch. We both cried on the bus ride back to the orphanage."

Bill walked into the family room and found us crying on the couch many times and would say, "Girls, don't waste tears on your mother. She is what she is and will never change. It was good you had the nuns in your corner, because of them you turned out great!"

He would give us both a big hug. My sister loved Bill. We both knew deep inside our souls time was very precious for both of us. In a few weeks we would be saying goodbye to each other. We feared my sister's life was slipping away and neither one of us could do anything to stop it. We talked about everything but dared not mention her illness for fear of the truth spilling out. She was dying before my eyes. It had been three months since her surgery, and she was frail and weak. She slept in my daughter, Suzy's double bed with her. Suzy was fourteen and took wonderful care of her aunt and godmother.

Sometimes I would wake up in the night and hear Suzy taking Jeanette to the bathroom. She was in so much pain, and she tried to convince me it was her nerve endings, which had been attacking her since the surgery. I knew it was different.

One night Suzy woke me. She was in a panic and said, "Mum, Aunt Jeanette is lying on the floor unable to get up."

Bill and I jumped out of bed and followed Suzy into her bedroom. Jeanette was curled in a fetal position and crying in pain. Bill lifted her up and put her on the bed while I called for an ambulance. The paramedics came within five minutes and took her to the emergency room at Mount Diablo hospital. Bill and I followed them in our car. We ran into the emergency room and was informed my sister had been whisked off to one of the rooms and had a doctor checking her. I got permission from a nurse to go to her since I was her sister.

She was lying on the bed too weak to respond to the doctor's questions. I wrote a note to the doctor and told him my sister had terminal cancer, and I didn't think she had long to live. She was visiting me from Chicago. He admitted her to the hospital and told me to contact her husband to come out to California since he felt her time was limited.

When I left the hospital, I looked at Bill and said, "I have to call Rusty to ask him to come out to California."

I cried all the way home. When I saw her boys and my girls waiting up for us with fear in their eyes. They knew by my face that the news was not good.

I looked at the boys and said, "I have to get in touch with

your dad. Your Mum is not feeling well, and you need to go back to Chicago, where she can be taken care of by her doctor."

I sat down on the couch and hugged both my nephews as my three children watched us with sadness, and words unspoken.

Rusty flew out to California the next day, and Jeanette was released from the hospital. She came back to the house to spend one more night. Jeanette left with Rusty and the boys the next morning for Chicago. When our eyes met, we knew she was dying. We both cried and hugged each other.

"I love you Maidy," she said as she and her family walked out my front door to a waiting taxi, to take her to the airport.

"I love you Jeanette," I said. "How can I live without you?"

Chapter 22

My Sister, My Mother, My Angel

My sister returned to Chicago on September 1, 1976. The next couple of months were devastating. I needed all the courage I could muster and hung on to my rosary and prayed for Jeanette and her family. I went back and forth to Chicago several times over that six weeks. I missed Bill and the children, but they were all very supportive during my time of need. I kept a letter my daughter Donna sent to me in Chicago, which has lived inside my passport all these years.

> Dearest Mom,
>
> All you have to do is read this letter every time you feel down, and I hope
> it will help you.
>
> God grants me the serenity to accept the things I cannot change.
>
> The courage to change the things I can.
>
> The wisdom to know that I don't have to please people all the time.
>
> Love Always,

"No two people have ever been so in love as my Mommy and Me."

Love you,
Donna Mariexxxx

It was very painful for me to watch my beloved sister waist away to eighty pounds. She died in early October as autumn leaves began to fall. I resented my mother as I had to pay for her airline ticket to Jeanette's funeral. She could afford to pay for her own ticket as she was working full time as a nurse.

She met me in Chicago, and we had to stay in a hotel together, since my brother-in-law did not want anything to do with her. Jeanette had told Rusty everything about our past, and the last time Rusty and Mum had seen each other they had gotten into a nasty scene over my sister and I having different fathers.

I said to Mum, "Is this true? Jeanette and I have different fathers, and Jeanette did not know?"

"Jeanette had no idea you had different fathers, but your mother lies about everything," said Rusty.

Mum looked at me and said, "Maidy, your father knew about Jeanette before I married him. He adopted Jeanette when she was born in London."

"Please Mum, I don't want to hear another word. Jeanette is my blood sister, and I don't care what you say any more."

When we went to the funeral home, Rusty hardly said two words to us, but I did speak to my sister's sons Christopher and Jamie. They were so sad at losing their mother, and I shared that grief with them both. When I saw my sister in the open coffin. I broke down and cried as I realized the finality of her death. She was laying on white satin in a wooden box looking serene. She was wearing the dress I picked out with Rusty. There were flowers everywhere I looked. Bouquets and wreaths with a sweet smell aroma spread around the room.

I wanted to climb in the coffin with her. She was my mother, my sister, and my best friend.

"Oh, God how am I going to live without her," I silently thought as I looked down at her.

I looked at my mother as she bent over her coffin, touching her face and saying, "I love you." I was angry and yet amazed to hear those words coming out of her mouth.

I stopped to think how many times she had said I love you to us as children, and I couldn't count the times on one hand. Suddenly, my anger was turning into an inner rage. How could she wait until my sister died to tell her she loved her? How could she place Jeanette in St. Marychurch when she knew her father was alive in London? The lies you tell will always catch up to you.

I wanted to scream at her, but nothing came out. I saw Jamie standing there staring at his mother with disbelief, and then he turned to me and said, "Mom had spaghetti before she died."

Funny, how spaghetti had become her parting meal on this earth. My thoughts flashed back to the orphanage and our visits to Mum on Sundays. Mum made us spaghetti on toast nearly every week before sending us back to the orphanage.

We went to the funeral the next day. First there was a solemn mass, which was attended by many nurses who worked with Jeanette at Little Company of Mary Hospital. We were driven in a black Cadillac car with Rusty and the boys, which followed Jeanette's coffin to the burial ground. I remember stopping at the traffic light and watching a couple of people cross the street in front of the car. They were both laughing. I wanted to roll down the window and yell at the top of my voice,

"Shut up, my beloved sister is dead!"

I wanted the whole world to stop and stand still because she was gone. When her body was lowered to the ground in a wooden casket, I finally realized she was dead. I would not see her or talk to her again. Death had become a reality. I had lost a sister, a best friend, and a mother. I looked over at my mother, and in that split second, my heart was saddened because she didn't know her daughter, my beloved Jeanette.

Jeanette had been a special part of my childhood. She gave me my first bicycle on my sixteenth birthday. I was working in Plymouth, during the school summer holidays in a children's orphanage, and she was doing her nursing training at the Royal Devon and Exeter Hospital in Exeter. She had saved a month's wages to buy me the bike, and she brought it down on the train to where I was working. It was for my sixteenth birthday. This was a two-hour journey, and she had to be back at work the same day.

Jeanette was always thinking of me.

When I first went to America I stayed at Jeanette and Rusty's apartment in Oak Lawn, Chicago. I was pregnant, and she watched over me like a mother hen until Bill came and took me to his home in Richmond, Virginia.

My sister called the baby Cookie. A few months later I lost the baby, and she shared my grief. She told me there would be more babies. When I got pregnant a year later, I had a beautiful curly haired girl, Suzy. Jeanette was her godmother, and she made her little dresses on her sewing machine. Everything that she touched was with love and care. My children adored her, especially Suzy.

When I look back over Jeanette's and my life, I realize that this was supposed to be the best part of our lives, where dreams we shared together finally came true. We both had our own home with a husband and children. We believed in God and attended church on Sundays. We both had good jobs in the nursing profession, but something went terribly wrong.

"Jeanette, you were not supposed to get sick and die."

A piece of my heart went with you, but life goes on and you must live in this world until the day you too will have to say goodbye.

I remember what you said to me in Marks and Spencer. I was 20 years old, and you were leaving to work in America.

"I will say goodbye and we will meet again soon as you are my sister never to be parted from me," she said.

That night Mun and I spent in Chicago, we both cried until we fell asleep. I said no prayers as I was angry with God, and I was especially angry with St Jude, who my sister prayed to for her life. He was supposed to be the saint of impossible miracles. There were no miracles to be found for my sister.

After returning home to California, my mother went back to England. I was thankful my girls were in school, but I had my three-year-old son to keep me busy. When I awoke the next morning, I took a long shower and dressed in my jeans and sweatshirt and decided to take a walk to the park with my son, Jimmy before my breakfast.

As I was walking through the park squirrels were running around us and leaves were blowing off the trees.

I said to Jimmy. "Grandpa and Aunty Jeanette are close by; I feel them. One day I will go to Mexico and visit Dad's home in Vera Cruz."

Chapter 23

It Seems Impossible Until It is Accomplished – Traveling to Mexico

I was walking along the golden sand, on the beach, and threw a pebble in the ocean feeling drawn to my sister. Did she go to heaven? Was she wandering around the earth as a spirit? Was she reborn?

"Oh God it is so hard to bring a life to a close. It is possible when you see it accomplished, but through you it will be done."

My sister and I had made so many plans after we came to America. We had planned a trip to Mexico to visit our father's birthplace, and when we retired, we were going to explore the churches and Museums in Europe. Jeanette would not get her chance to do so now. Ten years after my sister's death I decided to take my mother and brother to Mexico and see Dad's birthplace. Bill had taken me to Mazatlán for our wedding anniversary. This was a fun trip, and I wanted to go back to Mexico.

I thought my mother and brother would enjoy it as much as I had. Sharing our grief over my sister's death had drawn us a little closer together. Mum and Chris came through customs and met me at Los Angeles International Airport. They had come from Melbourne, Australia, where Chris lived with his wife and three children. Mum lived with her fourth husband, Geoff, a sweet man with a true Christian heart.

My brother brought my Mum to Australia after her last husband Owen died from cancer in England. He did me a service, as I could not have her stay with me in the United States. My brother and I were both thankful when Mum met Geoff in Australia, and they got married and moved into his home In Ballarat.

This trip to Mexico was a special trip for the three of us to discover and share the birthplace of my father and to get to know the Mexican people.

I gave Mum and Chris a big hug and said, "We are going to walk to terminal two and board the Mexicana flight to Mexico City. We have two hours before the flight leaves at 5:00 P.M."

Mum said, "I can't walk too far Maidy. My knee hurts."

"Don't worry, Mum, we will take two carts and you can push one to help you walk. Chris can push the other one."

As we walked to Terminal 2, Chris said, "I am really looking forward to seeing Mexico City and going to Vera Cruz where Dad's family had their factory."

I knew this trip was going to cost me some money, but my mother did not go near her purse when I was around her. I cannot remember ever being treated to a cup of tea or lunch from her which used to make me upset, but today I am much more mellow and have learned to curb my anger through the love from my children, friends and my two wonderful dogs, Marmite and Vegemite. I meditate daily through my spirit directly to God. This helps me tremendously with my O.C.D.

I looked at Mum and could see she was much slower in her walking, and more forgetful, but still had remarkable health at 74 years. I walked beside her and helped her push the cart into terminal two and we were on our way to Mexico.

We feared flying, and we had good reason with the Mexicana flight we were on. The airplane rocked and rolled all the way to Mexico City and it was pitch dark outside. We had no idea where we were. We sat on the edge of our seats and would not eat the meal but had a few drinks to calm our nerves. We were waiting to die.

The plane finally arrived at Mexico City with a bump and a screeching of the brakes as we landed. All three of us made the sign of the cross and Mum said, "Your father is watching over us."

I looked at my brother and said, "Were you scared?

He answered, "Yes, it was the worst bloody flight I have been on."

I laughed, and said, "Next time we will go first class!"

After picking up our luggage, we went to the bus station to catch a bus to Vera Cruz. My friends from Mexico with whom I worked told me there were two types of buses at the bus station in Mexico City. One is a rickety old bus which the locals take and the other is a big coach bus. I was told to get on the coach bus. Neither one of us spoke Spanish which made communication difficult. It was 9:30PM and this was an overnight trip from Mexico City to Vera Cruz.

I asked a bus driver who spoke a little English, "Which bus is for Vera Cruz?"

He pointed to an ugly beat-up old bus.

I said, "No," with my head nodding. "Grande Bus."

He said, "The grande bus is gone. No grande bus, in the morning grande bus. You go on that bus." He pointed to the old bus. It was scheduled to leave at 10:00 P.M.

I looked at Mum and Chris and said, "We have to get in line and get on the older bus."

My brother said, "I don't care. I am getting tired."

My mother looked horrified. She said, "Maidy, we can't get on that bus. Those people in line are carrying live chickens, and they will be sitting on the bus until morning."

"Mum, we have nowhere to go, and if we miss this bus we will be waiting until tomorrow to catch the next bus."

We climbed onto the bus, and our luggage was stored in their luggage rack with some live chickens. Mum and I sat together, and Chris sat on the other side with an old man carrying a cage with two chickens. I suddenly burst out laughing as I saw my mother clutching her bag to her chest. She would not put it down for fear of being robbed. My brother leaned over and told me the chickens were smelling and how long was the bus ride?

"We will not arrive until the morning around 6:00 AM," I said. The bus was full and there was a toilet in the back. I did not know if there would be any stops.

"Maidy, I can't use the toilet on the bus," Mum said. "I would rather wet my knickers."

Chris overheard her and said, "Mum, they have to stop for gas."

We laughed! It was pitch-black outside, and we could not see anything. There were no streetlights. My brother and I chatted back and forth, and Mum fell asleep with her purse attached to her chest. My brother and I finally drifted off. We were awakened as the bus started to rock back and forth and finally slowed down.

Mum awoke and yelled, "They're robbing us!"

"Mum," I said, "nobody is robbing us. The bus is taking a break. It is too dark to see outside."

My brother looked at Mum and said, "If these people could speak English, you would be kicked off the bus calling them robbers." The bus stopped suddenly and the driver stood up and beckoned the people to get off the bus. I could see lights and a gray building which looked like a warehouse. A large metal shutter was lifted, and I heard the music and saw people dancing. There was also a small service station with two pumps on the side.

Mum said, "It's 4:00 A.M. What is this place?"

Chris replied, "It looks like a Mexican nightclub."

I looked at Mum and said, "Go with the flow and don't make any comment. There may be someone there who will understand English, and we don't want to upset these people."

We went inside and there was a long food counter, a room with a table and chairs, and a dance floor. I followed my brother, and we started looking at the food which we had never seen before except for the tacos, enchiladas, and burritos. We pointed to the tacos and showed the vendor six fingers. We bought six beef tacos and three bottles of water. We walked over towards the exit and sat down at a table with four chairs. My mother was quiet and busy eating. She was staring at the people dancing.

Mum said, "People would not believe this back home."

Chris said, "Maidy, this is where truck drivers come and are entertained by these young girls that come here from the village."

Mum said, "They are prostitutes."

"Mum, you don't know that for sure," I replied.

At that time a big husky man came over to our table waving at me to come dance with him.

My brother said, "He wants to dance with you."

Mum said, "She can't dance with him. He might think she came up from the village."

"Thanks Mum," I said. "We could be related for all I know, and I will dance with him."

He led me to the dance floor, and we danced salsa. He was very light on his feet and smiled all the time we were dancing and said, "My name Roberto. You Americana?"

"My name is Maidy," I replied. "I'm British Mexican." We danced a second dance which was slow, and then he wanted a third dance, but Mum called out my name, "Maidy, we are leaving."

People were beginning to leave to get back on the bus, and I excused myself from Roberto and followed Mum and Chris out to the bus.

Mum said, "Thank God! I thought we were going to have to leave you here."

Chris laughed, and I shook my head. The bus drove along some bumpy roads, and I spotted a bus stop with a statue of the Virgin Mary.

Mum said, "I have never seen a statue near a bus stop. Have you Chris?"

My brother grunted, "No Mum, we will probably see St. Joseph at the next bus stop."

Mum laughed and clutched her purse close to her chest. We arrived in Vera Cruz at 6:00 A.M. We had not slept more than two hours and were tired. A service car from the hotel was waiting for us outside the bus station. A man was standing near an old Chevy with a sign.

Welcome! Maidy Gatewood.

"I guess that is me," I said to nobody in particular.

As we approached him, I said, "I am Maidy." I introduced my brother and mother.

He smiled and said in broken English, "Welcome to Vera Cruz. My name is Jose. I will take you to the hotel."

"Thank you, Jose," I said. "You speak good English."

He replied, "I study English at school."

We all got into the car and as we were driving I asked Jose, "Do you know a tour guide who would show us around Vera Cruz for three days?"

Jose asked, "What will you pay each day?"

I said, "$100.00 American dollars."

"I will be your tour guide, " Jose replied.

After he dropped us off at a beautiful Vintage Spanish hotel, I said, "We will see you at 11:30AM."

He replied, "Adios amigos."

Chapter 24

Daddy, I walk with Your Spirit in Mexico

We checked into the hotel, and each of us had our own room. Mum and Chris were delighted with their rooms, and this made me happy. It was 8:30 A.M, and we were hungry. We met in the dining room for breakfast. We love Mexican food and enjoyed all of the meals at the hotel. We all had chili relleno, eggs, and two chicken tacos with a cup of steaming black coffee.

I remember sitting in the hotel dining room and looking at the calm ocean all around us. At that moment I was thankful for being able to take my brother and Mum to Mexico. When I look back, I remember sharing some good times with them, especially touring Vera Cruz and Mexico City. This trip drew us closer together, but we could never talk about the past as Mum changed the subject immediately. I knew deep down she had many regrets, and I had learned to let the bad things go. She never once said she was sorry for her past actions.

We drank many margaritas and ate lots of corn chips while we discussed Cornwall and Devon. We had many good laughs! I remember one incident when we were swimming in the hotel pool and met a couple of older Americans who were swimming in the nude. It was in the late evening. I heard Mum say to the women, "Are you allowed to swim in the nude?"

The lady answered, "Why yes! This is Vera Cruz, and you can do anything that makes you happy."

When they got out of the pool Mum took her bathing suit off and swam around the pool.

She yelled out to me, "Maidy, take your swimsuit off. No one is here and it's dark."

"No thanks, Mum," I said. "You enjoy yourself. I am going up to my room, and I will be back soon."

After resting for thirty minutes, I came back down to the pool with my brother, who I met in the elevator. I told him Mum was swimming in the nude. He said, "Oh no, Maidy!"

When we reached the pool there were four young men searching for something, and we saw Mum wading in the pool.

She yelled out, "Maidy, I lost my swimsuit, and these young men are trying to find it."

One of the men said, "I found it. She tossed it in the flowerpot."

I thanked them, and they left the pool area. Mum put her suit back on and said, "I won't do that again." We all had a good laugh!

That night I laid on my bed gazing at the whitewashed ceiling and thought about my mother. We don't choose our parents, but I believe in respect towards them. Mum was too complex to understand. Within the last few years of her frail life, she told me how much she loved me and could not confront or apologize for the past. If I brought it up in conversation, she changed the subject. She spent the last years of her life in a nursing home in New Zealand. I visited her and paid her monthly expenses. She called out my name three times before she died.

"Maidy, Maidy, Maidy, where are you?" I was in California recuperating from hip surgery. I started to cry and picked up some pebbles to toss in the ocean, and looked up to the sky and said, "I have shed buckets of tears over you and Jeanette. Rest in peace."

Chapter 25

It is the Light Not the Darkness
that Gives Us Fear

England loomed large in my imagination, and I made every effort to remain connected to my homeland. Every vacation was spent in the place of my birth. I am returning once again to my beloved England, but I know in my heart this time is different. The box will flip open and spill many dark secrets that have suffocated me far too long.

As our plane flew over Scotland, a million thoughts were churning through my head. I gazed through the aircraft window, and in the distance I glimpsed at England through rolling clouds drifting into the morning sunlight. They were the color of charcoal, tipped with white ash and streaks of orange resting on patches of blue sky. I looked for one shining star. *Somewhere, some place my beloved father is watching over me.*

The captain turned on the seat belt lights, and the flight attendant announced over the speaker that we would be landing at London Heathrow, in fifteen minutes. I could barely hear the grinding sound of the wheels as they dropped down from the British Airways 747 aircraft for landing.

I blocked my ears from ringing. Suddenly we started our descent towards Heathrow Airport, one of the busiest places in Europe.

The rolling clouds had dissipated. A sunrise was breaking through shedding a golden glow over England. I was mesmerized by the panoramic view I saw from the aircraft. As we got closer, I could see patchwork quilts of rich green and golden meadows surrounded by tall old gothic buildings and red brick houses clustered together.

It was a smooth landing. The seat belt lights went off, and everybody stood to collect their carry-on luggage, and quickly formed a line to wait patiently to exit the plane.

I could feel the tears pricking my eyes with thoughts of returning home. I exited the plane, pulled out my British passport with pride, and walked down the ramp towards immigration. After showing my passport to the officer, he greeted me, "Welcome home."

This made my day. I picked up my luggage and walked through the green exit. I went up a ramp into a throng of people who were waiting for their family and friends.

No one was waiting for me. I went directly to the Tube station and climbed on the train bound for Waterloo station.

After arriving at Waterloo, I transferred to the Eurostar train, which would take me to Belgium, to visit my father's grave in Leuven, and then I would return to England.

I had booked a seat in first class, which was only half full. Feeling jet lagged, I sat down in my reserved seat close to the window and rested my weary head on the pillow. I was sitting in a four-seated area with a table in the middle, and two seats were unoccupied. A young man dressed in blue jeans and a gray sweater sat opposite me with his head bent down reading a book.

The train chugged slowly out of the station, and I closed my eyes. Finally, my journey begins. I am going to visit my father's grave. In my dreams, I saw a little girl with outstretched arms running towards a man. She suddenly stopped and wiped tears from her eyes with the back of her hand. It was me, running towards my father. Sometimes I see a young woman walking with an older man along the seafront. She stops to pick up pebbles and toss them one by one into the ocean. It was me with my father.

These images have haunted me throughout my life, giving me joy and torment as part of discovering who I am. I have crossed two continents where my family is scattered to discover my family history. My father's story began a world away in Mexico. The story told by my great aunts was that my father's mother died in childbirth.

After my aunts died, my brother told me our grandfather had a torrid love affair with one of the factory workers and got her pregnant with our father.

My grandfather took my father from my grandmother because she was not good enough for his family.

He raised my father until he was seven years old, but he died suddenly of a heart attack and my great aunts went to Mexico and brought my father to England to raise him.

My brother said, "Mum had told me that dad believed his mother was still alive and one day he will go to Mexico to find her."

The aunts raised him in the Christian Science religion. They wanted him to be a practitioner in their church, but he had different plans; he yearned for his freedom. At nineteen Dad moved to London where he attended University of London to study business, while working part time. My Aunts cut off his allowance when he told them he would not join the ministry. He was happy with his independence.

My father worked at the Clarence Hotel in London as their Maitre d' in charge of all of the other waiters. He met my mother, Edna May Coad, when she applied for a waitress job at the Hotel. He hired her as she told him she was in nursing school, but needed to work as she was pregnant and the father did not want her or the baby. They worked five months together and my father fell in love with Edna. He wanted to take care of her and the unborn baby. They got married at the registry office in London, attended by a few friends from the Hotel.

My mother's family were not happy with the marriage. They were both prejudiced and considered my father as a "half-cast." Auntie Wilhelmina, my mother's sister, told me that my grandfather worried about gossip from the neighbors because Daddy was Mexican. Even though my father was an educated man, my grandfather would not accept him. My Uncle Mick told me, Dad took great pride in his Mexican culture, but he loved England and adopted it as his country.

My sister Jeanette was born in London. My father adopted her as his own daughter. I found out she was my half-sister before her death in 1976.

Mum said, "My father loved her dearly."

My brother, Christopher, was born two years after my sister. Due to the outbreak of war, my parents moved to South Devon, to be close to my grandparents. My parents loved Devon, and they thought it was a nice place to raise a family.

Devon has many charming villages, which are bound by red cliffs and thatched roof cottages. John Keats, the poet, had a summerhouse in Teignmouth, Devon.

He was quoted as saying, "Here all the summers I could stay."

Devon has extensive sandy coves with a history that breathes through the gothic buildings that are standing to this day. During World War Two. Many refugees from London were evacuated down to the Devon countryside. Our climate and country air was considered healthy for the children, and many families in Devon volunteered to take the children in their homes.

According to Mum, my father loved Devon. It reminded him of parts of Mexico. My parents settled in Exeter, an ancient city that is the gateway to South Devon. They lived a block away from my grandparents.

My grandparents were of Irish and Cornish descent. They

were the fiercest of people with hot tempers that my mum and her siblings had inherited.

Mum said, "When your Grandpa lost his temper he used his leather belt to beat her."

Everyone in the village knew Mum's family, the famous Coads.

Their neighbors feared them. As long as I can remember, I have held a great admiration for my Irish grandmother. She was a stubborn, religious, Irish Catholic, who led an independent life. She had physical disabilities she acquired in midlife.

During wartime Grandma had a knitting group. They knitted scarves, gloves, and hats for the refugee children. They called themselves "The Clickers." Wool was a luxury, so Grandma would entice the neighbors with ration coupons for sugar and sweets to give her their old woolens. The Clickers would rip old woolen sweaters to provide yarn for the group. Through my grandma's Irish blarney, she would tell the future to people at the local pub with a regular deck of cards. She read my cards when I was twelve years and said,

"Maidy you will marry a foreigner like your mother and leave England to live in another country."

"Will I have children?" I asked.

She answered, "You will have two girls and two boys."

Her predictions all came true. I met and fell in love with Bill Gatewood, an American serviceman stationed in Swindon, where I was doing my Nursing training at the Royal Air Force base.

As grandma projected, I have lived most of my life in America. I had four children Two girls and two boys. One boy, Mark Antony, died in my sixth month of pregnancy. This was a sad period in my life.

Grandma loved her Irish whiskey. All of her children adored her. When Grandma died, Mum gave me her honey pot container. It was brown and yellow with a little bee on top of the lid. I keep my bobby pins in the pot. It has a couple of hairline cracks, but that does not bother me. Today, I regard it as one of my treasures.

Grandpa was born in Cornwall. His family history goes back to the Jamaica Inn, on the misty moors in Bodmin. His history and tales are connected with pirates coming during the night from the Cornish coast and bootlegging whiskey.

Grandpa was a captain in the army and was proud of his British heritage. He graduated from Sandhurst Royal Army Military Academy. He was a tyrannical man with a hot temper. He ran his family home like a barracks. Mum spent her early childhood in India where grandpa was stationed in the Army; she was the second to the youngest of four girls with three brothers. Mum adored my grandmother and hated my grandfather.

Mum told me when she was eighteen, Grandpa pushed my grandmother down a flight of stairs in a heated argument, which resulted in a broken hip. Grandma was confined to a wheelchair until the day she died. This was done in a fit of jealousy as my grandmother had many male admirers whose company she enjoyed at the local pubs. Grandpa was drunk with beer and whiskey when this incident happened.

Mum told me she was attending nursing school in London when she got the message from Uncle Les that their mother was in an accident. She returned home immediately and barely spoke to her father. Grandma was a great cook and made fruit pies that would melt in your mouth. My favorite were her Cornish pasties.

Over the years grandma became an alcoholic. She continued to wheel herself down to the pub each day and drink with her friends.

She died when I was thirteen years old.

I admired her. My Irish grandmother was stubborn with the strength of a lion, but was a woman of great knowledge and substance. Mum never spoke to grandpa from the day of her mother's accident. She said her father broke her mother's heart.

Years later Grandpa was admitted to the Royal Devon and Exeter hospital where my sister Jeanette was doing her nursing training. He came into Jeanette's ward on a rainy afternoon, and only by his name did she realize he was our Grandfather.

She contacted me in Swindon. My sister told me Grandpa was ill, and she asked me to come and visit him before he went home. The next day I caught the train from Swindon, eighty-two miles from London, and three hours on the train to St. David's Station, Exeter, Devon. I had not seen my grandfather since I was twelve years old. I went straight to the hospital and saw a very sick old frail man, who had cirrhosis of the liver.

When he looked at me, he said, "You look like your father, and you have your mother's Irish eyes."

I stood there until he fell asleep. When Jeanette got off duty we went to a restaurant close by and had a plate of fish and chips. Over a cup of tea, we both started talking about Grandpa.

Jeanette looked at me and said, "Maidy, Grandpa is an alcoholic."

I answered, "I know, like grandma and all Mum's brothers, and our cousin. What is wrong with them?"

"They love booze and women," she answered.

We both laughed and left the restaurant.

A few years later Grandpa died at my cousin Irene's cottage in Lyme

Regis, where Irene had taken care of him.

Irene and Les are my favorite cousins and all of my family love Irene's son, Craig. They have always welcomed us into their home in England. I am glad I got to know them in my early twenties by forming a bond with them while babysitting my daughters, Suzy and Donna, when I visited England. I can thank Mum for introducing us.

I loved Irene's parents, Aunty Joyce and Uncle Les. They loved my father and filled me in on many details of his life.

My family has enjoyed some wonderful Christmas dinners at Craig and Irene's home. Irene is a wonderful cook and makes her own Christmas pudding and cake, which are the best I have ever eaten.

She took great care of Grandpa, Uncle Les, Aunty Joyce, and Craig Sr. before they passed away. Irene is a great person and a wonderful writer. I love her, Craig and Les, dearly.

Chapter 26

Searching for Identity

My eyes opened to a sudden jolt. The train was changing tracks and slowing down. I looked out the window and it was pitch black outside. I knew we were heading through the underground tunnel towards Brussels.

The Eurostar arrived in Brussels on time. I stood up and put on my coat. I could feel the chill of the cold from the outside with winds bursting through the cracks around the windows. I reached for my luggage and got off the train. On exiting the Eurostar station, I showed my passport and proceeded through the station to catch the train to Leuven. The train was waiting on platform eleven.

It was pelting down with rain. This was a very old train but the seats were comfortable. I felt extremely tired as this was a long trip to take in one day. When I got on the crowded train, I felt the wet rain drop on my hair and shoulders which I brushed off as I found a window seat and sat down.

I tried to see out the window through the mist and fog, but it was impossible through the heavy sheets of rain.

As the train started to move, a trolley appeared laden with sandwiches and beverages. I bought a cup of tea and a tomato and cheese sandwich, which I scoffed down immediately followed by my hot cup of sweet tea. When the dining cart returned I bought a custard tart, which I had my eye on when

I bought my sandwich. The waitress offered me a refill on my tea; I gladly accepted.

I started to drift in and out of sleep with my thoughts trailing towards my father, wondering how he felt flying in the night raids across the British channel, back and forth to Germany, during World War II.

Mum said, "Dad hated dropping bombs on Germany. He had many

nightmares of children screaming."

She said, "His greatest fear was that his family would not survive a German air raid."

My thoughts went to the letter Daddy wrote to me before he died. It was an incredible testimony with his loyalty towards England and his family and friends.

My mother kept the letter in a wooden box in her bedroom, and I took the letter and a photo of my Dad in uniform. I was leaving home to join the Royal Air Force nursing school, and I wanted a photo of my Dad. My sister Jeanette took me to Mum's town house while she was at work. I picked up a few clothes which Jeanette gave to me. My mother never mentioned Daddy's letter before. Thank God, I found it when I was looking for a photo of my father.

At that time I still had a lot of anger built up inside of me towards my mother. She never wanted to talk about my father. When she was in her senior years, she talked to my children about her family and my father.

I thought of my father with love and admiration, but there was much confusion and pain, which overwhelmed me. I thought of the time my Uncle Mick, Mum's younger brother, told me he was with my Mum when she received the news of my father's death.

She knew the moment when he was killed!

Uncle Mick said, "It was a cold, wet night, Maidy. You were a baby, and you were staying with your grandparents. My uncle was reading his book in the early hours of the morning in the kitchen. Everyone was sleeping when suddenly he heard a blood-curdling scream from Mum's bedroom.

"Fernando is dead. My beloved Fernando is dead." My grandmother and my uncle rushed to her bedroom. Mum told them she had a dream that she had seen my father's broken body lying beside a smoldering airplane. His uniform was torn and bloody. She had woken to him calling her name at three o'clock in the morning. She knew my father was saying goodbye to her. The next morning a telegram arrived from His Majesty's Service. It was brief.

A German Fighter had shot down my father's plane over Hamont-Achel, a small town on the border of Belgium and the Netherlands, at three o'clock in the morning on June 16, 1941. There were no survivors.

Condolence from His Majesty, King George VI.

He was on his way home on leave to celebrate his baby girl Maidy's birthday, on June fifth.

He had flown his missions and was ready to come home.

But fate dealt a cruel blow, and I lost my beloved father. He had volunteered to take the place of a man who was too sick to go on his mission.

That night was his last.

In later years through the wonders of technology, my son, Jim, who is a historian, gathered the following information in the beginning of the twenty-first century regarding my father's death.

On the 16th June 1941 between 2250 and 2305 hours, seven, two-engine Wellington bombers of the 103rd Black Swan Squadron took off at Newton Air Base in the English county of Nottinghamshire. Their mission was to bomb the harbor installations at the river Rhine in Duisburg.

For this purpose each plane had enough load on board. Three 500 bombs with direct ignition, one 250 pound bomb with delayed ignition and 6 "units" with 4 pound incendiaries. On the night of 16th to 17th June 1941 the Wellington –bomber N2849 of the Royal Air Force crashed in Belgium in the town of Hamont (north-eastern part of Belgian). The complete crew of six lost their lives.

My beloved father was killed. Did he suffer?

Oh God! You knew there would be so much tormented suffering for his loss, and the devastation it will leave for his family for years to come? God, Oh God! Why my father?

Flying those war missions to Germany must have taken so much courage to face the enemy. What went through his mind on his return home to England? Did he think of all of us? Was he thinking about coming home to see his Maidy and the family?

Oh, Daddy, it must have been dreadful for you not knowing whether you would return to England. Behind closed doors I have shed buckets of tears thinking about the night your precious life was taken from you and wondering what it was like when your airplane was shot down over Hamont and blown out of the sky.

When I was a little girl, I would search the sky for that special light, and in a flash he came into my heart. I spoke to him from my soul. I saw my father sitting on a big fluffy cloud bathing in the moonlight watching over me. When the stars came out at night I saw a cluster of angels, soaring towards earth, bringing my father to me. The sky would light up, and a ray of warm sunshine would engulf my very being.

One night when I was at Marychurch, I remember lying on my bed gazing at the stormy gray sky. The rain was beating against the dormitory window. Suddenly, I heard a loud noise of thunder with a flash of lightning. I jumped up on the bed to look out of the window and watch the lightning flash across the sky. Tears flooded my eyes. I was upset because Daddy was outside in the thunderstorm. I could not see any angels in the sky. It was pitch black. The only light shining was a lamppost with its dull light.

When I went back to bed, I tossed and turned all night thinking I won't see him again. I prayed to the Virgin Mary to give me strength. I said, "What will I do if I lose contact with my father?"

In the early morning, after the storm had ceased, I could hear the birds chirping and rustling in the trees. I looked outside my open window: everything was fresh, and clean. There was a beautiful rainbow streaking across the sunlit sky.

I believed my father created the rainbow just for me. I wanted to reach up and touch it with my fingers and make a wish. Oh, how I would wish that my father would come down to earth and spend some time with me. I would ask him to take me far, far, away to Torreon, Mexico, and show me where he lived as a little boy.

Suddenly, the sound of a loud voice woke me up, "Tickets please, tickets please." The conductor was hovering over my shoulder, waiting for me to show my train ticket. It was in the book I had been reading.

He looked at my ticket and said, "Leuven is the second stop."

I leaned back on my seat, and I pressed my face against the window. I felt the coldness on my head as I looked into the night. Once again, I thought about my life and how lucky I was. To have good health, a great job, three wonderful children and my dogs, Marmite and Vegemite.

I am now fulfilling a long time dream in writing my book. What more could I possibly need?

Deep within my soul I thought I had shut the doors of my past, but they were wide open from many years spent in dark shadows with so many questions and no answers.

Looking out the train window I could see a sullen gray sky, and noticed a light mist had set in. I watched the trees gently swaying in the wind as they flashed by me. The rain seemed to have subsided, but drops were still trickling down the window pane like parachutes dropping from the sky. The sheep had clustered under the chestnut trees, reminding me of cauliflower laid in rows in the fields ready for the farmers to pick.

The train moved at a steady pace chugging along the railway tracks in the silence of the night. I saw the graceful form of every stark denuded tree, and watched the branches waving to me as I passed them one by one. Fields separated by a sparkling stream, went flashing by as I strained my eyes to see where its winding course would end.

My joints were beginning to feel stiff. I got up and stretched my legs, and walked to the dining coach. I bought a cup of tea and some digestive biscuits, and went back to my seat. The tea was strong and tasted good but the biscuits were great! I was beginning to feel restless. My OCD was acting up, and I was overwhelmed with my brain thinking of the past and going to see my father's grave once again.

The train had slowed down to a crawling pace, and I could see the Leuven sign in the distance. People were getting up and putting on their coats and hats, and getting themselves ready to exit the train. The train suddenly stopped a mile away from the Leuven station. We had to wait for another train that was heading towards us to pass by. I could see the platform in the distance. It was shiny and slick from the rain and glistened in the light. I buttoned up my coat and pulled my hat around my ears.

I stood by the train door and I could feel the cold wind streaking through the cracks. It was a biting cold which entered my body leaving a dull ache in my joints. The train started to move very slowly, and then there was a sudden jolt. The train had stopped. The lights of the station lit up the darkness of the night, and people were anxiously waiting to get off the train

I stepped down onto the platform and breathed a sigh of

relief. I felt a strong presence of my father, and in my heart I knew he was expecting me.

I thought of an English proverb: *"Let every man praise the bridge he goes over."*

I felt like I accomplished this when I arrived in Belgium.

I felt a glimmer of fear in my heart as I stood on the platform knowing how close we were to the German border. I had never traveled in that direction, but there will be a day I will go there.

There has been too much time passed without some act of forgiveness by me towards the German people. I have spent a lifetime listening and sharing a vengeful hatred of the Germans.

In the past it has been extremely hard for me to converse with German people without hostility or believing that they killed my father. We think of prejudice as a contemptible act, but each of us has a little prejudice in us, and some people have a whole lot more. Family prejudice can carry from one generation to another as it did in my family.

Chapter 27

Courage, Strength, and Hope

Leuven is a quaint village surrounded by magnificent architectural buildings. I never get tired of walking through the village and looking at their art history, especially in St Peter's Church where a figure of Christ's head sits carved from the twelfth century. This piece of art is one of the most precious in Leuven.

There are many churches in Leuven, which are predominantly Catholic. The Catholic University is one of their biggest attractions. Students come from all over the world to study at this university. I picked up my luggage and walked towards the exit. The train station was small and on the outskirts of town.

There were two cabs parked outside the station. I waved to the first one and he pulled up beside me. He got out and put my luggage in the car boot, and I got into the back of the cab. As we drove off into the night, I told him to take me to the Holiday Inn, and he nodded his head and proceeded through the village to our destination. We passed a row of old mellow brick houses with mossy roofs. This was a familiar site as I had taken this route a few times. We turned left and I could see the brick house on the corner with an inset of fieldstones and a garden sprayed with lilac, which was draped over the white picket fence. I rolled down the window to get a whiff of the scent, but the air was too damp and cold.

I felt a great sense of tranquility all around me. I gazed out the car window and was enchanted with the Christmas decorations and lights flashing in the shop windows. I saw the trees that lined the main street. They were clustered with tiny green and red lights giving the village a warm glow.

In the distance, I had a panoramic view of tall white gothic churches, which dated back to 1487. They were a sight to behold. This was the Christmas season. Carol singers were standing outside wrapped in their warm winter coats, singing to people passing by the main square. I could see the empty manger as we passed the center of town, signifying the birth of Christ. As we came closer to the Holiday Inn, I saw the oldest gothic building, which was the Catholic University. They had a library dating back to the eighteenth century. Leuven is one of Belgium's historical landmarks, and the people that live here are very proud of their village and traditions.

I passed my favorite bakery which I often visited when I came to Leuven. The bread sits in quaint wicker baskets in the shop window; they are crusty and delicious to eat, especially served with butter and jam. Their pastries are tempting and a treat to the palette. Next door to the bakeshop is the popular *Frites* place where the teenagers hang out. I could never acquire a taste for their French fries, but my children loved eating them when they visited Leuven. The french fries are dipped in mayonnaise and put in a cone shaped bag; they call it *"freetos."*

I leaned back in my seat and drank in the peace and serenity all around me. I especially enjoyed my visits to my father's gravesite. I come here every other year around Christmas. This place never changes, only the people getting older.

I arrived at the hotel hungry, exhausted, and ready for a good night's sleep. I took my luggage up to my room and came back down to the lobby and walked out the front door to find a place to eat. I eventually stumbled on a cute place, with a

Parisian atmosphere. People were sitting at tables outside in the cold, wrapped in big overcoats and wearing gloves and hats. I decided to go inside. Within five minutes after ordering my dinner, I was sipping wine, and eating a delicious Italian meal. I especially enjoyed the crispy bread, and melted butter that came with the meal.

My table was close to an open fireplace. I sat there in my big comfortable chair and watched the flicker of the flames as I sipped my red wine. I could hardly keep my eyes open thinking about the events facing me tomorrow. I love visiting Leuven, but my top priority for being here was to visit Daddy's grave. As I glanced at the families eating around me, I thought of my son Jim and my two daughters, Suzy and Donna. I felt a deep pride and appreciation towards them and for their encouragement and support in writing my book. I missed my children especially now they have all left home and have their own lives to live.

After dinner, I took a shortcut back to the hotel. I walked across the cobblestone village square surrounded by the gothic gray buildings. You could sense the mysteries of years gone by. The square was wet and slippery from the rain, but I enjoyed the dampness in the air and the spray of rain upon my face. I felt like a young kid on a field trip, in awe of the architectural buildings that stood so stately in the square. I passed by the Catholic Church and made the sign of the cross and went back to the hotel.

As I walked through the lobby, I said good night to the lady at the front desk and went to my room. I turned the television on the BBC channel to listen to the news and went into the bathroom and had a hot shower. With my bath towel wrapped around me I opened my suitcase and pulled out my nightclothes. I slipped into them and my body felt warm and comfortable. I turned off the television and got into bed.

I lay there wide-awake within the cool sheets watching the stars peeking through the window. The soft cotton cream curtains were fluttering as a light wind came through the window.

I listened to the silence of the night and asked God,

"What did he want me to do?"

Deep in my soul I knew the answer. I was to continue my journey with courage and conviction. I tossed and turned for a good hour. Finally, I got up and went outside onto the patio.

The trees in the front of the hotel had Christmas lights wrapped around them which flickered as they swayed in the breeze. It had stopped raining, and the reddish sky was sprinkled with stars. I went back inside and fetched a towel from the bathroom and placed it on the patio chair and sat down. I looked up at the stars and then closed my eyes. He knows I'm here. I feel the strong presence of his spirit. I opened my eyes and looked longingly at the stars and said, "Daddy, are you there?"

My thoughts wandered back to my childhood. It was at an early age when I knew Daddy had been killed in the war, but I never knew where he was buried. His name was not mentioned. If I asked any question about his family, it would make my mother become agitated. When I joined the Royal Air Force and entered nursing school, I did my own research and discovered that my father had been buried at the Royal Air Force cemetery in Leuven. It was my twentieth birthday before I could pluck up enough courage and money to see Daddy's grave, but now I visit often to seek the comfort and serenity I desperately need from him.

I remember the first time I flew to Brussels, the capital of Belgium. I felt as if a cold clammy hand had touched me at the airport.

I stayed in an old century hotel on the outskirts of town. The room had a dismal atmosphere, which depressed me. There was a musty smell in the room and the walls were dark and dingy. A picture of an old man was hanging above the bed. I looked at him staring at me; his eyes were cold as steel, with a grim look on his face. He had a salt and pepper beard with a pipe in his mouth draped on his lower lip. I thought he might be a friend of Hitler's so I covered the picture with a pillowcase.

The darkness had set in outside, and it scared me to leave the room. I felt hungry and called the front desk and asked them if I could have my supper delivered to my room. They obliged me with a tray serving the night's special, which was roast beef and mashed potatoes, carrots and peas with gravy and a pot of tea. I remembered to remove the pillowcase from the picture when my supper was brought to me, but when the door closed. I put the pillowcase back on the picture.

After I had eaten my supper, I turned on the television and was relieved to tune in to the BBC. I watched the news and then walked over to the window. I drew open the yellow lace curtains and saw a ghastly moon peeping through the dark clouds. The street in front of my window looked like the back of a solitary churchyard. I could feel a cold dampness in the air and visualized Adolf Hitler standing with his top men in front of this very window planning the destruction of Europe.

I closed the curtains and stayed up most of the night reading and writing in my journal. After three hours of sleep, I woke to the sound of hoovering outside my room. I dressed and went down two flights of stairs to the dining room. I sat down at a little table in a dark corner.

A crisp white tablecloth covered the table. On the table sat a pot of tea and toast rack with four pieces of white toast, and two little jars of jam. The hotel offered bed-and-breakfast, and this was the breakfast they served with the room. If you requested anything extra, you paid for it. I was happy with the toast and tea. After breakfast I checked out of the hotel and took a taxi to the station and caught the train to Leuven. And here I am back at the Holiday Inn, my favorite hotel, sitting on my patio.

Chapter 28

We Will Meet Again with No Tears

I vividly remember the Royal Air Force cemetery in Leuven. It was located in the countryside. I took the local bus from the village square and was dropped off half a mile from the cemetery.

I walked down a long winding country lane, where small red brick houses peeked behind long drooping willow trees and mulberry bushes on each side of the road. After walking a half-mile, I stopped short in the middle of the lane to rub my eyes.

There it was, a panoramic view of the Royal Air Force cemetery. It was breathtaking. When I got closer, I could see tall trees standing stately in the background and hear birds singing in the branches of the chestnut trees. Trees spread over the entrance gate.

I saw a big squirrel scurry by. It was a deep reddish color with bright beady eyes. There was a cottage situated on the right side, closer to the cemetery, with the front lawn strewn with rich green clover. On the left was an old farmhouse where a plump lady, with a checkered scarf wrapped around her head, was hanging her laundry on the washing line. I waved at her, and she waved back.

I could see cabbages and cauliflowers peeping up through their vegetable garden, and there were horses standing close to the fence watching me as I walked by. I picked up a big rosy red apple from the ground that had dropped from an apple tree, which was hanging over the blackberry bushes on the side of the lane. I bit into the apple and the juice quenched my thirst.

I reached the front gate and stood there transfixed by my surroundings. I felt like I had stumbled into a rainforest where white square tombstones stood on attention to the sound of raindrops and the whistling of the wind through the trees. I thought of the long waiting period of where two souls would finally commute together.

There was no gravesite in England. No real proof of his death. Nobody in the family wanted to talk about him, especially where he was buried.

Every day I expected him to walk through the front door and pick me up and tell me how much he loved and missed me. But that was a dream, and this was a reality.

I pushed open the squeaking white gate and went over to an alcove on its left side. There was a tattered book resting on a wooden shelf. I picked it up and flipped through the pages. It was the register, and there were very few signatures in the book. I signed the register. "Daddy, I'm sorry it took me so long to find you. I am your beloved daughter, Maidy. I love you."

I looked on the map for the location of my father's grave, and began the long journey to find him. I walked along a stone pathway, past many tombstones of servicemen and stopped to check their ages. I was astonished by their age. There were many men younger than my father buried there.

I was overwhelmed thinking of how many families had lost their loved ones, and how many mothers had lost their sons. Many of the fallen ranged from nineteen to my father's age 26 years. I stood for a few minutes, and looked directly over all the graves in the cemetery. My eyes filled with tears, and I prayed for all these lives lost in a senseless war.

And for all the broken hearts and children left behind. I continued my walk and found his tombstone in row E. I stood in front of the grave just staring at the white stone square, with his name scrawled on it. The day he died, and his birthday. It seemed so cold, but I knew in my heart it was the reality of his death. I felt like screaming, "No! My father is dead! My father was killed in the war. I hate the German people."

There was nobody else in sight. I was alone in a cemetery, a burial place for pilots and their crew. I paused and looked at the long line of graves. What struck me, was that all these men were young boys who had sacrificed their lives for England. I sat down on my father's grave and sobbed for him and all the other fathers, and sons, whose bodies laid here in this cemetery,

Through my veil of tears, I noticed a large reddish squirrel standing by the headstone. I watched him as he ran up and down. I stood back a few steps as the squirrel perched himself on top of the headstone, and in a quick flash I realized this was a sign that my father's spirit was close.

I felt the pangs of pain deep within my soul for what my father had endured when his plane was blown up in the darkness of the sky. My eyes became fixated on the crew members buried beside him as I looked at their names in silence. War had destroyed these human lives, leaving their family and friends with broken hearts and shattered memories.

The Belgian people have taken good care of the cemetery. I stooped down and dug up the earth in front of the tombstone with a dinner fork that I had taken from the hotel. I planted a variety of English flower seeds in front of his grave. I then knelt down on the wet grass beside his grave and closed my eyes and prayed and waited until I could feel his spirit joining my spirit. We communicated through our souls.

I poured out my heart to him, telling him things I couldn't share with anyone except my sister and children. I told him how life had been one big struggle to grow up without him, and how hard it was for me to love and trust another human being. I told him I didn't blame him. I was proud of him for his courage and strength, but I asked him why did he have to die when so many fathers came home?

I sobbed many tears that day and told Daddy I had so much anger towards Mum for putting Jeanette and me in an orphanage after he died. I was a baby, and she left me there until I was eleven years old. Tears were burning my eyes, and I couldn't cry any more. At long last I was beginning to feel closure for his death. I wiped the teardrops from my eyes with a big handkerchief that I carried for these moments. I got up off my knees and walked towards the gate, but I kept looking back expecting to see Daddy follow me.

I opened my eyes and felt a warm sensation once again. This is my father's spirit circling around. I have come back to visit you again and I will see you tomorrow.

The moon that faced the Holiday Inn was bright, lighting the clouds with a white glow. I looked up and saw a light in the sky and knew Daddy was close by

"Oh, Daddy, I have missed you so much, and thought of you every day of my life. It has taken me a lifetime to forgive the people responsible for taking your life, and even now I don't know if I truly feel the forgiveness in my heart."

The light in the sky became brighter. Tonight was special. The angels were watching over me. I thought about my sister Jeanette who died of cancer when she was thirty-nine years of age. She was so young, and I miss her so much. I wondered if she was with Daddy and watching over me. I have had sadness in my life, but something unexpected has always appeared around the corner to encourage me, and give me added strength. I believe God has been my greatest inspiration.

I felt exhausted and went inside the room and climbed into bed and fell asleep.

The sound of water awakened me running in the adjoining room. It was 8:00AM. I jumped out of bed and turned on the television to watch the BBC news.

Scattered showers today. I will need my umbrella. I jumped

out of bed and went into the shower. I like taking showers in the Holiday Inn as they have big fluffy towels, and the soap gel smells like flowers in springtime. I dressed, grabbed my bag and umbrella and went down to breakfast.

Breakfast at the Holiday Inn has always been a special treat for me with the fresh fruit, yogurt, a variety of cheeses and breads, and homemade jams served on a buffet with hot porridge, eggs, and bacon.

I entered the dining room and sat down at a table for two and was greeted by the waitress, who asked me what I would like to drink, and did I want toast with the buffet?

I answered, "Please bring me some hot porridge and some coffee."

I got up from my chair and went to the buffet table and fixed a bowl of mixed fruit. I looked at the array of different cheeses and could not be tempted this morning.

I enjoyed the hot porridge. My appetite was smaller than usual. I was nervous, thinking about Daddy. After breakfast I called for a taxi and went to the cemetery.

As we drove through the town, shops were opening their doors for the early Christmas shoppers. Umbrellas were bobbing everywhere, and you could see the rain pouring down splashing and dripping in the puddles on the wet ground.

The church bells chimed at ten o'clock; Mass had started. I made the sign of the cross as we passed the church. I wondered how many masses I had attended in my lifetime. I have always had a passionate loving relationship with Jesus, and I have raised my head to the sky many times in search of him.

I noticed a flower shop on the corner, and I asked the taxi driver if he could pull over to the shop as I needed to buy some special flowers to place on my father's grave. I spotted a variety of wild English flowers, colors of the rainbow covered with wet droplets. I purchased a bouquet, some holly, and mistletoe. They breathed a fresh spring aroma everywhere, which made me sneeze.

As we passed the main cathedral, I bowed my head in silent prayer:

Oh Lord Jesus.

I pray for peace. War destroys everything.

Chapter 29

Remembering the Past
Creates New Beginnings

In the distance I saw the Royal Air Force cemetery with its backdrop of tall lush green trees. This was how I remembered it the first time I was here. As we reached the cemetery, I could see the graves covered by a leafy carpet of scattered leaves of amber-yellow, gold, and red, looking like quilts of many colors.

Headstones were standing erect in formation as if they were ready to march. I could hear birds chirping from the trees in sight. The cab driver dropped me off in front of the little white rickety gate. As I opened the cab door I could hear the birds chirping from the trees.

I pushed open the gate and went over to the brick alcove, where I signed the guest register. My son and I were the last people who had signed last year. I walked towards my father's grave and placed some fresh flowers on each crew member's grave from his flight. The rest I placed on the end of his grave. I bent down and pulled out the dead flowers from the soft rich brown earth. I wiped off the headstone with my handkerchief and pulled out the flower seeds I brought with me from America. I reached in the bottom of my purse for a spoon and dug around the earth. I touched the soil tenderly as I placed the flower seeds in the dirt.

Standing, I wrapped my arms around the headstone. The rain was spitting on my face. I felt fresh and clean. I was thinking about my son Jim. I remember when Jim and his friend Charlie went to Mexico in search of his grandfather's roots.

It was last summer. Jim returned home and said, "Mum, I feel much closer to granddad. Especially when I was in Torreon, his birthplace. It was almost like he followed me from the time Charlie and I arrived in Mexico, watching over me."

I answered, "You are probably right, as I feel that same emotion when I visit his grave site in Belgium."

My uncle told me many times that Jimmy was very much like his grandfather in looks and personality. I have always felt that part of my father lived in Jimmy. I strongly believe what God has taken away he will give back to you.

My eyes welled up with tears. I felt the anger bubbling up inside of me again, for losing him to a death caused by war and hatred. I knelt down on the wet grass feeling a need to be close to him. The cemetery was quiet and solitary, shadowed by the dark gray clouds in the sky.

Suddenly from nowhere once again appeared the reddish brown squirrel I had saw the day before. He ran up and down the headstone, paused, looked at me and ran to the nearest tree. Jim and I had seen a squirrel when we arrived the last time we were here. I knew in my heart, somehow, this was an acknowledgement from my Dad.

I talked quietly to my father, telling him all the family news. I was releasing my inner emotions, from times gone by. It saddened my heart for the years we had been apart and yet so close. I wondered if he could hear me and feel my relentless pain.

The quietness and peace circled around me and rendered my soul to the depths. I love you Daddy and I will always love you, but I will never comprehend why God chose you to die.

You were so young and so courageous to give your life for England, and I am proud of you.

You did not die in vain because you have lived within my soul, and when I take long walks in the cool of the evening, and hear the chirping of the birds in the trees, I know you are close by. Somewhere I lost my childhood, but when I'm with you in spirit I feel like a child, because you listen and understand the child within the woman.

I can laugh and cry with you and express my innermost thoughts, even though you don't answer me. I know you're there beside me watching over me. The letter you wrote before you died is from a man of courage and conviction; for this special legacy I humbly thank you. I pulled out the folded letter, covered with a plastic cover, from my purse and read it once again:

My beloved daughter, June (Maidy),

Please understand Daddy did not want to go to war and leave you, Mummy, and your brother and sister. Interpret my death as God's alternative in showing my love and devotion to England, my family and my friends.

Through the outcome of this sacrifice, my loved ones and England will be free. In dying, I have lost more or as much as other men who fought this war. In life God blessed me with good health, a sound mind, and a loving family. You, my beloved daughter, and your brother Christopher, and sister Jeanette, were my crowning glory and a gift from God. When you walk outside in the cool of the evening, you will hear birds chirping and see squirrels scrambling from the trees. You will look up to the sky and watch the stars, knowing I will be close by. You will pick wild flowers and hear the whistle of the wind, and our souls will lock as one.

Remember, Maidy, you were conceived in love and great passion. Give this love to others, treat people with respect, and forgive those who anger you. Find your purpose in life, and do everything in moderation. As you grow from child to woman, seek what life has to offer, as learning is continual. Believe in God. Pray to God, and take care of your mother.

We will meet again, in another place where tears and pain will be a fallacy, and smiles and laughter one unending symphony.

Daddy loves you so much.

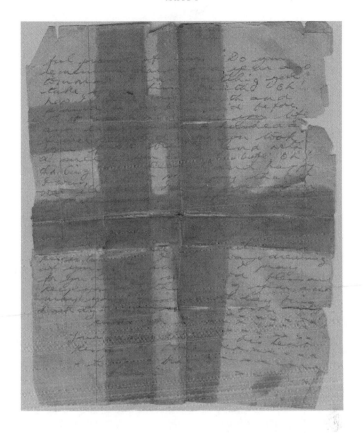

I have read your letter as equal to saying the Lord's Prayer, and each time I feel the strength and passion of love for our family between the lines. I have reached for this letter at my lowest ebb for support and courage to oversee any obstacles that have encompassed me during my life.

With you, Daddy, I was somebody. You lit up the room when I felt your presence. My birth was no mistake, you wanted me, but you got killed, and in dying you have left behind part of you inside of me.

I wiped my eyes from the burning tears rolling down my face. I looked up and saw a bright light. It was flashing through the tall trees that were standing gracefully in the back of the cemetery. It suddenly stopped flashing. In that magical moment I wondered if this was another sign from Daddy letting me know he was close by.

As I started to walk from my father's grave, I thought about all the young men buried in this cemetery. Each one of them had sacrificed their lives to defend England. I knew at that moment when I died, I wanted my ashes taken to Devon by my son, at the right time. The place where my life began.

I turned my head to look back one more time. Daddy had spent his last gray days.

Flying among the clouds so high
        Those that I fight I do not hate
Thoughts are for whom I love
        Knowing I shall meet my fate
Drove to this battle in the sky
        Balanced between life and death
No cheering or waves goodbye
        Years to come one wasted breath
Balanced wings brought to mind
        While other planes are winging
The fear of that desperate climb
        I see the gray seas shimmering
In infinite light a moon swam low
        At night winged engines sail
Half seen shadows flicker to and fro
        The winds outside scream and wail
Watchful eyes and ears that strain
        A shattered sound from the guns
The crash of bombs around my plane
        Flying against these nameless sons
A sudden silence! In the sky
        As I fall downward bound
           Star of peace rise high
             My soul the angels found

I thought about the angels. I know without a shadow of doubt everyone has an angel to guide them through life. Because I was raised by Catholic nuns, I have deep spiritual roots, which have been my umbrella and guidance. I strongly believe that everything is possible through God and prayers.

Chapter 30

Time Brings All Things to Pass

I took a deep breath and started my walk from the cemetery, down the long country lane heading towards the village shops. Trees bordered the fields on either side of the lane and their tops waved with the wind. I can smell the damp leaves that have dropped off the trees and scattered on the ground. When the leaves have turned yellow and red, the sky turns a deeper blue splashed amongst the white clouds. The leaves on the ground make a crackling sound as I tread on them. I look down and see clumps of wet leaves circled around the trees and bushes. I kicked the leaves around smiling at the thought of the little girl still inside of me.

I walked past a thatched roof cottage which was buried in a wooded area. The front garden was crammed with an array of different colored flowers and tea roses intertwining around a white picket fence. The rose petals were sprayed across the walkway leaving a sweet aroma. I realized at that moment the meaning of "stop and smell the roses."

I stood for a moment, and leaned against the picket fence. I could hear the birds twittering as they nestled in the thick branches of the chestnut trees. I took some deep breaths and touched the wet ivy trickling over the fence. Today is my special day to be free and breathe the pure country air. I felt young and healthy again.

I walked towards the village and stumbled on a quaint restaurant open for lunch. It was a tumbledown cottage with slate steps that led to the entrance. I almost tripped over a plant pot as I entered the front door. There was a rosy glow about the place. An old couple greeted me and seated me at a round table with a checkered red tablecloth and a comfortable cushioned chair to sit on.

I was the only customer and had the couple's full attention. The old man spoke broken English, so I could communicate with him. I ordered vegetable soup with an egg sandwich and a big pot of tea. It was raining lightly outside and the weather was cold, but there was a nice warm fireplace close to my table. My food arrived. I was fascinated by the delicate bone china dishes, especially the teapot covered with a flowered tea cozy. It reminded me of my mother's violet teapot, but hers was cracked. I inherited the teapot, with a story to tell.

The cracked teapot traveled
            Across the Atlantic Ocean
From Devonshire, England
            To the United States
Digging deep into the box
            I pulled out the violet teapot
From the shredded white paper
            Wrapped around the china belly
It looked the same, except
            The spout had a hairline crack
I remember Mum dropping it
            As I announced to the family
I was dating an American G.I.
            She had a fit as the pot fell
It spun like a top on the kitchen tile
            Leaving a crack on the spout
"This belonged to your grandmother"
            She yelled.

I clutched the teapot to my breast
       It was fragile and light
I tilted the lid, looked inside
       To see dark brown stains
With spider-web cracks
       Remembering family teatimes
Tears, arguments, and beatings
       Like me, the teapot survived
The teapot has now retired
       It sits on my bookshelf in America

I gazed into the fireplace and poured another cup of tea, which I enjoyed in solitude. I watched the burning coals in the fireplace. I thought about my children. They became silent when I talked about my childhood. I know in my heart my past saddened them. I have always encouraged them that through God and motivation we can face any obstacles that might prevail through our lives as we never know what tomorrow might bring. I am so proud of their compassion, strong independence, fortitude, and living their lives to the fullest.

I left the restaurant and waved goodbye to the old couple who had wide grins on their faces, perhaps due to the tip I left on the table. The rain was spitting down my face, and I quite enjoyed it. I walked slowly back to the village. I stopped and watched the cows munching the wet grass, unaware of the patter of the rain; I pulled my hood over my head and walked at a faster pace. As I walked down the narrow cobbled streets, I noticed everyone carrying their umbrellas except me. I saw the snowdrops in the garden of an old brick house on the corner.

The flowers were swinging on their thin green stalks like drops of frozen snow and were spreading onto the sidewalk. I reached down and picked one up with my gloved hand and pressed it in my journal. I smiled thinking back to my childhood picking primroses with my sister when my old maid aunts took us for a country walk. They would point out the fresh buds of snowdrops and crocuses to us, but we loved the dandelions.

I remember the time I saw a dog heading my way. I cried and hid behind Aunt Susanna's long knitted skirt because dogs scared me. I never understood why because as an adult I loved animals, and I am now the owner of two wonderful shih-tzu dogs, Marmite and Vegemite.

The rain was coming down at a steady pace. I took cover near a shop window under the awning which protected me from the rain. After the rain subsided, I continued my walk back to the hotel.

I stopped at the Catholic Church. I gazed at the statues in the church. I was overwhelmed with its gothic architectural beauty, dating back to the fifteenth century.

The church had high arched ceilings and a breathtaking tabernacle that presented a superb panoramic view from the church pew. I knelt down in front of the altar; I reached in my bag and pulled out the holy rosary and prayed on the beads. When I left the church, I stopped at a fruit stand, and bought some red juicy apples and immediately munched on one.

I smiled thinking of my aunt's cottage, Nogales, in Devon. My sister and I loved playing in the back garden as it was full of fruit trees. When the apples grew plump and ripe we would pick them off the trees. When they hung green and unripe on the trees and it rained, we would lick the drips of water from the apples, and this upset our aunts. There were blackberry bushes that grew big plump blackberries after we picked them. My aunts made delicious apple and blackberry pies, which I loved with hot custard. These were happy memories of my childhood.

I walked back to the church and had the urge to enter it once again. As I walked down the aisle, I felt the Christian faith that the nuns had instilled in me. God is my daily bread and has been the instrument of my courage and convictions in life. To believe in God is to know him.

God has been my friend and guidance during my life. When I listen to my inner soul in silence, I know He speaks to me. Once again, I knelt down in the pew in front of the altar and bowed my head in prayer. I thanked God for many gifts he has given me in my life, especially my three children and five grandchildren.

I said, "Please God, protect my children from harm and help me guide them through a Christian life as you have gifted me."

Leaving the church, I could hear the clock strike three o'clock. The rain had stopped. I walked down a narrow street near the town square, and came across two big iron gates open to the public. I walked into the courtyard, and I could see in the distance a beautiful garden. As I got closer, I realized it was a park, with a duck pond in the center, surrounded by wooden benches where people were sitting enjoying the afternoon.

I sat down on the grass under a weeping willow tree, where clusters of clover were peeping through the falling leaves. The afternoon air was cold. I could hear the distant laughter of children playing in the park. I lay on the damp clover and was delighted with my utter solitude. I gazed up into the sky through the tree branches. The clouds hung low. I closed my eyes and fell asleep. The sound of the rustling of the leaves from a squirrel running past me awakened me. Darkness had set in. I jumped up and looked at my watch. It was five o'clock. There was a winter cold chill in the air. I walked briskly until I felt warmer, and then I walked at a slower pace as I made my way back to the hotel.

When I returned to my room, it felt empty. I took a shower. The water felt good running down my back, and I felt refreshed after a long day. I thought about Daddy's gravesite in Leuven. I will never tire of visiting it as I feel this is a powerful connection to my father. I want my children to see their family history. I want them to know that war brings devastation and finality to families that are left behind.

If we cannot learn from our past, there is no future for us. I will not forget my past, knowing I lost my beloved father and was snatched from my childhood. I turned the shower off and reached for the bath towel and wrapped it around me. There was a chill in the air as I dried myself. After I got dressed, I looked in the mirror and a solemn face was looking back at me. I smiled and put on some makeup to make me feel better. I turned on the television and lay back on the bed to listen to the news from the BBC station.

After the news I jumped off the bed and put on my boots. I suddenly heard a voice outside in the hallway and then knocking on my door. It was the maid delivering some additional towels I had requested. After she left I made the decision to take the train to Brussels for dinner. I bundled up and made my way from the hotel to the train station.

The weather was freezing outside. I had two sweaters under my leather coat, but I could still feel the chill as I pulled my knitted cap over my ears. The train for Brussels was boarding as I arrived at the station. It was crowded, and I found a seat near the exit door.

I arrived in Brussels station within one hour, and then took a taxi to The Grand Place, which was the city's forum, where the tourist population go to eat and shop. I found a cute restaurant that served British food, and felt happy that I had come here. I ordered roast lamb, mashed potatoes and vegetables with red wine. There were few people in the dining room, but that did not bother me as I have learned to enjoy my company.

After I had eaten, I walked around the Grand Place. This was the heart of Brussels, where the medieval buildings swept you back to the days of powerful guilds and barons. It's Flemish Renaissance-style buildings dated from the late 1690s. This was a merchant trading place. I walked past a tall Gothic building, which was the Hotel de Ville. The belfry was off-center, and the building itself had an off-center entrance arch which was built this way on purpose.

I exited The Grand Place and stumbled in a tavern with a long name, Poechenellekelder. I went inside and saw the largest collection of puppets. The place was alive with people and puppets. I sat down at the corner table, a waiter served me a glass of red wine, and I kept on staring at the puppets. I was thinking how much workmanship had gone into them because they were so detailed and lifelike. As I waved goodbye to the puppets, I hailed a taxi and took the train back to the hotel in Leuven. That night I fell asleep as soon as my head hit the pillow.

Chapter 31

Haunting Memories, Dreams Linger On

I awoke at 1:30 A.M. in a cold sweat, from a turbulent dream in a terrifying atmosphere. I was on a double- decker train, which had stopped in Germany at dawn. In the distance I heard the shrill of a whistle and then a loud voice ordering me to get off the train. I stepped off the train onto the platform and suddenly realized I was the only one standing there. The train left the station, and by a powerful force I was pushed through the exit door towards a German village in Hamburg. All I could see was a big sign that said, "Welcome to Germany, Maidy."

I was abandoned in Hamburg, Germany. I walked around in circles trying to go back to the railway station. I felt tired and hungry, but there was no place to eat or buy food, and there was a strange silence everywhere. I cried and suddenly yelled, "Help! Help!" There was no response. Suddenly I heard the shrill of a siren, and the grinding sound of airplanes. I looked up in the air and saw the Royal Air Force bombers straddled across the evening sky, dropping bombs all around me. Death was a possibility. I ran for cover under an old Oak tree in a nearby park.

I yelled at the top of my voice, "I am not a German! I am British."

The grinding noise of the airplanes drowned out my voice. Suddenly, the bombs stopped falling, and the roar of the engines ceased, only to be replaced by a mocking laughter from the German people that had become visible to my eyes. They were gathered in groups around the park and some were sitting on wooden benches.

I yelled to them, "I hate you! I hate you!"

They yelled back, "Your father dropped bombs on our country, and killed our people and our children. He is a murderer! Why are you still living? We hate you!"

I ran, picking up my pace as I listened to their screeching voices and the patter of their feet behind me.

"Your father killed German people!" These people were my demons. Nobody could see them but me. My breathing was deep and shallow, and I could feel my heart pounding in my chest. Finally, I could see the train station ahead of me. The door opened, and I sprinted into the station almost tripping over some bricks scattered in the entrance. I was determined to get away from the Germans. I ran to the platform where a train for Brussels was waiting to depart. I jumped on the train and hid in the toilet until I heard the shrill of a whistle. I woke up and suddenly looked at my watch. The strap was sticky from sweat, and the time was 1:30 A.M.

I sat up in bed and spoke out loud several times, "It was a dream. It was only a dream." This was my OCD, my anxiety acting up once again. I have had many frightening dreams since childhood. I rolled out of bed and crept into the bathroom. I sat on the edge of the bathtub sick to my stomach, consoling myself that this was a figment of my imagination. I stood up and walked over to the mirror and touched my cold cheeks and washed my clammy hands. I sponged my face with a damp washcloth, and I went back to bed. I lay there with my eyes fixated on the white chalky ceiling while dark shadows flashed around the room.

The curtains were open. I had forgotten to draw them completely. The moon was full and bright and shined directly on my face. My eyes glistened from the tears that had welled up from deep inside. I prayed to the Lord Jesus to give me courage and strength and to make these dreams and death demons go away.

I thought about the word forgiveness, and what I would say in silence to the German people. "I forgive you for destroying my family. I forgive you for blowing up my father's plane. I forgive you for starting this war. I forgive you for making an orphan out of me. Will I ever forgive you for taking my beloved father from me?

"No! No! No," I whispered to no one in particular. Eventually, I drifted off to sleep.

Life is a burning light
       Glowing day and night
There is no time to waste
       Decisions made in haste
Tomorrow may never come
       Leaving things undone
A future lies before you
       For dreams to come true
Like a sheet of fresh snow
       With marks that will show
On the hills you climb
       And roads that whined

Characters are built
       In a patchwork quilt
On the twists and turns
       And experiences we learn
Different roads we seek

And souls that we meet
Through courage we grow
Seeds planted to sow
Along the winding trail
We succeed or fail
Grief and doubt left behind
Treasured memories unwind
Maidy

I woke the next morning early. I wanted to catch the early train to London so I could be home before dark. I decided I would take a taxi to the station and eat breakfast on the train. I had a quick shower and slapped on some face cream. I brushed my long hair, which was still damp. I placed a green knit cap on my head and went down to the hotel lobby.

I had ordered a taxi the night before, and it was sitting outside right on time. I got into the car; I wrapped my scarf tight around my neck. We drove along darkened roads where the cobbled streets glistened from the rain and the streetlights. There was a delicate veil of mist covering the village of Leuven. We arrived at the station, and I had five minutes before finding myself sitting on the train heading to Brussels.

In the distance I heard the drumming of the train wheels striking the rail joints. It was 7:30 A.M., and as we left the platform, I noticed it was crowded with people going to work. Everyone seemed to be in a hurry and carrying umbrellas except me. I was wearing a warm raincoat and had covered my head with a woolen hat. I intended to spend most of the day on the trains traveling back to London.

When the train came to a stop, many people bustled forward to get off. I sat near a window, and I had a seat to myself. I watched the people climb onto the train carrying newspapers and sack lunches. I was thinking about how people are the same all over the world with their daily work habits.

The train moved slowly out of the station, and I knew I was

finally on my way to Brussels to catch the train to London. I lay my head back on the pillow and felt a surge of nausea coming from the pit of my stomach and knew my anxiety level was high. There had been many days of rootless uncertainty about this trip, but I had to accomplish my own. I yearned for my sister's company. I also wanted to be alone, without my children. I did not want them to know how deeply my childhood had affected me. They were back in America.

My son had a strong connection with my father and through an internet search had helped me to uncover additional knowledge of my father's family history. Jim often reminded me that this was my journey to continue writing my book, and it was one I needed to take alone. Pushing my thoughts aside, I looked out the window and saw trees and fields running alongside the train. The fog had lifted, but there was a gray darkness amongst the clouds, which showed rain. I saw the sheep huddled against the trees and envied them for their life of solitude.

The train was pulling into the next station. I watched people get on the train dressed for comfort and warmth. When the train moved, I made my way slowly to the bathroom. As I sat on the toilet, I looked at my face in the small mirror and saw beads of sweat on my brow from my never-ending anxiety. I washed my face and hurried back to my seat. I looked at my watch and realized we had traveled for almost one hour. The next station would be Brussels. I reached in my purse for the train schedule back to London and decided I would catch the 12:00P.M. which would get me into London at 3:30PM.

I said a prayer to the Lord Jesus to give me the strength and endurance I needed for my mind and body to deal with my OCD. I thought of the prayer of Saint Francis and quoted it silently to myself.

Lord, make me an instrument of your peace:
where there is hatred, let me sow love;

where there is injury, pardon;
where there is doubt, faith;
where there is despair, hope;
where there is darkness, light;
where there is sadness, joy.

O divine Master, grant that I may not so much seek
to be consoled as to console,
to be understood as to understand,
to be loved as to love.
For it is in giving that we receive,
it is in pardoning that we are pardoned,
and it is in dying that we are born to eternal life.
Amen.

The train started at a slow pace and gradually picked up speed. Green fields were flashing by my window, with cows and sheep spread over the fields for miles. Occasionally I would see old buildings, which were probably farmhouses as we were in the Belgium countryside. As we headed into Brussels, the trees turned into thick bramble bushes with berries and dandelions popping in between. The sun was breaking through as some clouds were dissipating. Brick houses appeared which were hidden behind the tall trees. I pressed my face against the window to look at the vegetable gardens in the back of the homes. I could see the cabbages and cauliflowers standing in neat rows. They were close to the railway tract. My mind churned back and forth, and I carried my head like a block of cheese. I felt stronger but mentally tired after my trip, and I was looking forward to going back home to England.

Chapter 32

You Will Never Reach Your Destination If You Stop

I stepped off the train onto the platform, and a cold wind swept over my body. I wrapped my scarf around my neck and pulled my green hat over my ears to prevent me from catching a cold as I followed the other passengers who were walking through the exit to catch the Eurostar train to London. I quickly glanced back at the train, which was leaving the station.

I could hear the voices saying, "You will be back. You have to come back and make peace with the German people."

After checking in at the Eurostar terminal, I stepped into the first restaurant and found a table in a corner and ordered a sandwich with a mug of coffee. I watched a young family eating their lunch together and thought of my children and how much I missed them. They were my greatest gift from God. I am so proud of all three of them. I made the sign of the cross and thanked God. People have often asked me why I became a Catholic, and I would tell them, "I think of religion as one God, and my Catholicism came from my upbringing by the nuns when I was orphaned at Marychurch." Why am I still a Catholic? Why change? We all pray to the same God, but in different ways.

What echoes in my heart, especially when I am feeling low,

are the words of John Henry Newman, a theologian and an Anglican priest and later a Catholic priest and cardinal:

> God has created me to do him some service; he has committed some work to me which he has not committed to another. I have a mission. I may never know it in this life, but I shall be told it in the next. I have a part in a great work. I am a link in a chain, a bond of connection between persons. HE HAS NOT CREATED ME FOR NAUGHT. I shall do good, I shall do his work; I shall be an angel of peace, a preacher of truth in my own place, while not intending it, if I do but keep His commandments and serve Him in my calling.

As I was draining my coffee mug, I could barely hear the loudspeaker announcement. Passengers were to line up to catch the Eurostar to London. I took my time as I had a reserved seat and did not want to get caught up with crowds of people. I left my mug on the table and walked towards the train.

"Finally," I thought, "I am on the way home to England."

I was seated in first class near a window and noticed the compartment was empty. This was good news as there were no train stops before London. As the train started chugging out of the station, I noticed how quickly it picked up speed. This was a three-hour trip and I was mentally exhausted from delving back into my past within the last few days in Belgium. There were only a few days left before Christmas, and I planned to stay in London for one night before flying back to Los Angeles to spend Christmas with my family.

I wondered if my children understood the pain I have endured over the years. I knew I had obsessive thoughts and anxiety problems, but when I was growing up I could never speak of this subject to anyone. There was no medication to resolve these problems, and if you were to show any signs of mental illness, they locked you in a mental hospital.

I remember during my childhood, whenever I got angry, I banged my head up against the wall until it hurt. I felt like I had a crack in my brain and these voices were spilling out into my mind telling me I had to bang out the anger to overcome the devil; I would then pray on my rosary for forgiveness.

I rested my head back on the seat and fell asleep. I was awakened with the loudspeaker, announcing we were arriving in London. When I exited the station, my first reaction was a sigh of relief. I got into a taxi and went to the Paddington Hilton, my favorite hotel. When I entered the hotel lobby, I could feel the nostalgia of Christmas around me. The hotel was brightly decorated for the holiday season. There was a large Christmas tree with a shining white star on top, sitting in the center of the lobby, with bright-colored Christmas gift boxes underneath the tree.

After checking in, I went on the elevator up to my room, and when I closed the door behind me, I felt that sinking feeling of nausea in my stomach. I was utterly alone. I lay on my bed and could hear voices in my head saying, "You have to go back to Germany; your father killed the German people!'

I stood up straight and walked over to the window and faced the people across the street with tears falling down my cheek and told them in muted silence.

"I cannot forgive you for killing my father, and I will never forgive Hitler and his Nazi regime for the atrocities they committed to so many people."

When I listened to these voices, I felt like I was going mad. I gazed at these people standing across the street and suddenly realized they were like me. I wondered if any of them had endured pain the way I had. I felt a lump in my throat and cried.

"I hate renting brain space to these voices. Will they ever go away?"

"Please God make the voices go away".

I thought about my mother and brother, who could never discuss what happened during the war. It was through my aunts, uncles, and the Royal Air Force that I finally learned about my father. My brother, Chris, felt nothing for Daddy. He blamed Dad for joining the RAF and putting himself in harm's way when he wasn't required to do so. Because my father had not been born British, he did not have to join the Service.

My brother said, "I have no time for him. You don't leave a wife and three children."

I never discussed Daddy again with Chris or Mum as it hurt me too much. I was born into a family with secrets, but I knew the truth. My dad didn't have to go to war. He volunteered his services trying to help a country that he loved and was proud of. He didn't want to die, but he sacrificed his life for England.

Mum never visited my father's grave in Belgium until I brought her there with my three children. The trip was too expensive for her, but she had gone to Paris a few times over the years. When Mum went to his grave she knelt down on his coffin and wept bitterly. The children and I left her her for fifteen minutes. When we were leaving the cemetery, Mum kept thanking me for bringing her with the grandchildren on this trip to Belgium and visiting Dad's gravesite. I saw her vulnerability for the first time. We shared a bond with my father. She loved her grandchildren and told them what a great grandfather they had missed. He would be proud of all three of them. At that moment, I felt some forgiveness towards her and made a silent promise to my father that I would take care of her needs in her older years. I did follow through.

My thoughts were churning regarding my parents. When I look back, I thought maybe they were too young to experience such a tragedy. Like many young couples, they had dreams, but the war ripped them apart. Mum said, "Daddy was the love of her life."

When he died, part of her died with him, and they left us

children with crumbs. The love in our family died when my father was killed.

That night I took a long hot shower. I let the water run down my back for half-an-hour and washed my hair. I needed to feel clean once again. The bath and the shower had always been my refuge when I needed to be alone and think about everything.

The time was 5:00 P.M. and I was feeling hungry. I got dressed and went out to eat my fish and chips in Paddington station. I spent time browsing around Paddington shops to pick up some Christmas gifts. The men in our family were easy to buy for as they needed warm sweaters and socks. I found a department store that had everything I needed. Marks & Spencer's. I bought some sweaters for my beloved son and then went to the socks and underwear department and purchased some warm pajamas and socks for him.

I felt worn out with the shopping and made my way to the store restaurant and plopped myself on a chair. The waitress came over and took my order for a pot of tea. As I waited for my tea, I saw two little girls dressed alike. They sat on the other table, and I asked them how old they were? The mother answered, "Two and four."

I thought about my girls, Suzy and Donna, two years apart, and I had made their little dresses and dressed them alike. My girls were so precious to me.

"Where did the years go?'

It seemed they would be around forever. I remember how we loved to go into San Francisco by train and spend the day shopping and eating lunch out. They are grown up with families of their own, and I treasure the moments when I see them, especially with my grandchildren. Donna has a beautiful daughter called Mackenzie and a handsome boy named Evan. Todd is her husband and they are soul mates.

Suzy, my eldest daughter, had three handsome sons, Chris, Nicky and James, whom I love dearly. She is married to an Australian, Justin, and they are very happy. They live in Australia.

The server bought my tray of tea and set it on the table. I wish my girls had been able to come and join me in London as they loved shopping here. If I am lucky, there will be another time. As I was drinking my tea, a lady came over and said something in Italian, and sat down on the chair opposite me. I did not speak Italian, and she did not speak English. We sat and drank our tea in silence. In Europe it is not unusual for a stranger to come and sit at your table. I got up from my chair and smiled at the lady; she smiled back, and I went to the children's department.

I searched in the children's dresses and found a soft pink dress for Mackenzie. After purchasing the dress I asked the lady where I should go for the boys' department? She pointed in the direction in the back of the store where I found four warm sweaters for my precious grandsons. I was laden down with packages, but the hotel was close by and it was not long before I walked back into the hotel. I dropped my packages at the front desk. I had to go back out to buy another piece of luggage to carry the extra stuff I had purchased for Christmas gifts.

I walked by the shops looking for luggage. I felt spiritually close to my father. It was almost like he was following my footsteps. I often looked back over my shoulder expecting to see him, especially when I heard the rustling of the trees from the strong winds that lined up and down the street outside the railway station. I saw a man-selling luggage and purses out on the sidewalk, and I stopped and purchased a bag large enough to carry my gifts and two purses for my daughters.

I went back to the hotel and picked up my packages and went up to my room. I threw the shopping on my bed, looked at my watch and went back out to the pub across the street from the hotel, as my OCD had been acting up, and I needed to get away from demons that pestered me. I walked over to the pub and could feel the warmth of the local people as they were clustered together around the fireplace. I sat down at a heavy wooden table and listened to the echo of jovial voices and laughter all around me.

A ruddy-faced man serving drinks behind the bar spoke to me with a Scots accent, "Lassie, what do you want to drink?"

I answered, "Do you have Beefeater Gin?"

"For you Lassie, I have anything you want."

I smiled, "I would like a gin and tonic."

After a few drinks I sang Christmas songs with a group of people who had come over to sit with me and were extremely friendly. People like to communicate and ours was through laughter and a song. We didn't know each other's names, and there was very little conversation, but here we all were having a great time. One lady asked me what part of England I come from as my accent sounded different.

"I come from Devon," I said.

She shrugged and started singing Christmas songs and I joined her. After waving goodbye to everyone I left the pub at 10:30 P.M. I walked towards the hotel lightheaded and happy. I fell asleep as soon as I got into bed. I woke up the following morning with a slight headache, tossed some clothes on and walked out of the hotel to go to an early mass at St James church. It was a block away from the hotel. I wore my heavy jacket as it was damp and wet outside.

I arrived at the church and was pleasantly surprised with their beautiful Christmas decorations. I prayed on my rosary as I followed the mass. The priest was young and had a deep Irish accent. I slipped out of mass after I received Holy Communion. I walked back to the hotel and stopped in the dining room for a continental breakfast.

When I returned to my room. I turned on the television to watch the news. It was cold and wet in London with continual rain throughout England for the next few days. I had a quick shower, dressed and packed my suitcase. I called the front desk for a cab to the airport. Suddenly, the phone rang, and I answered it. Jim was on the other end of the line wishing me a Merry Christmas, and I returned the greeting. I told him I missed him and I was leaving for the airport and would see him soon. He was already at home for his Christmas break from UCLA where he was attending college. I said goodbye to Jim. No sooner had I put the phone down. It rang again, I answered the phone and it was the front desk, to let me know my taxi had arrived for the airport.

It was raining outside and as the porter was putting my luggage in the trunk, I climbed into the back seat of the cab. My ride to the airport was twenty minutes. I sat back and stared out the window at the Christmas decorations and the London people.

The umbrellas were like balloons flopping around in circles. Traffic was busy but much slower due to the wet weather. I watched the red double Decker bus, I smiled thinking of the many times I had ridden on them, and missed them living in California.

We arrived at the airport and drove directly to International to catch Virgin Airlines to Los Angeles, California. After the cab driver loaded my luggage in a basket, I went to the Virgin desk for business class and checked in for my flight. I had one hour to spare and went directly to the gate where we would fly out.

As I approached the gate people were lined up, and I went through to the business class line and got on the plane. I had a good flight as I slept most of the time, and watched movies. I enjoyed the comfort and good food in business class and some gin and tonic.

My plane landed in Los Angeles at twelve midday. I was happy to be in America, my second home, and to see my family and friends. I attended Christmas mass the next morning, and after mass I walked over to see the Christmas manger. The miracle of birth is the miracle of life, and through the kingdom of heaven there is a miracle after death to come.

"This I believe!"

As I closed my eyes that night, in my dreams, I could hear the rhythmic drumming of the train wheels striking the rail joints softly saying,

"England, I smell the flowers, I smell the sweet grass, and I can feel the winds on my cheeks."

"I must go back to England"
The country of my birth
      To pick the wildflowers
            And touch the rich earth
I must go back to England
          To the village that I know
Spread on the rugged hilltop
          You can hear the wind blow
I must go back to England
          Touch the berries growing wild
Seeing purple violets in the field
          Once picked by me a child
I must go back to England
          In the summer or spring
Where tall trees turn velvet green
          And birds nest and sing
I must go back to England
          To walk on cobbled streets

Maybe I'll play hopscotch
          Or run on my bare feet

I must go back to England
                        And feel the raindrops fall
I must go back to England
                        My country with great pride
In history and honor
                        We will walk side by side
Maidy

Healing the Past

"Like chains shackling me to the past. I will no longer pollute my heart with bitterness, fear, distrust, or anger. I forgive you because hate is just another way of holding on, and you don't belong here renting space in my brain anymore."

Beau Taplin

On December 16, 2018, I finally went to Germany with my son, Jim, and his beautiful wife Patricia. It was the dead of winter and we were on our way to Hungary where we would take a weeklong cruise on the Danube. It was a special trip organized by Patricia to celebrate my retirement. We flew from San Francisco on Lufthansa Airlines to Frankfurt, Germany. The service was excellent and it was a smooth flight but a bumpy landing.

We arrived in Frankfurt in the wee hours of the morning in the pouring rain. After going through customs, we found the airport was practically deserted. We were flying on a connecting flight to Budapest and had a couple of hours before the flight took off. Jim and Patricia left me with the luggage while they scouted around for some coffee. I sat down and watched the sunrise with the rain pelting down outside the big windows. I was cold and lightheaded with my mind running in circles.

Was I here sitting at the Frankfurt Airport in Germany? A place I would never have considered visiting. Germany has taken so much space up in my brain as I have spent most of my life hating its people and blaming them for my father's death and destroying our family.

I stood up, walked towards the window and looked outside. It was desolate. I pulled away from the window.

"I can't forgive you!" I thought. "Not only for England, but the atrocities you committed to the Jewish people and prisoners of war." As I went back to my seat, Jim and Patricia were walking towards me with coffee and snacks.

Jim said, "Mum we will have to move. We are at the wrong gate for our flight to Budapest."

We gathered all our things and made our way to the new gate. People were already boarding the plane. I stood there looking at the people and felt uneasy as I never thought I would board a German plane with German people, but here I was with my son and his wife going to Budapest.

Jimmy said, "Mum, are you alright?"

"I cannot believe I am here in Germany," I whispered.

We boarded the plane, and I had a glass of orange juice as I was feeling lightheaded.

I looked at Jim and Patricia. "I didn't think Germany would affect me this way," I said. "Some of these people are my age."

Patricia answered, "This has been a long trip for all of us and we can rest when we get to the hotel in Budapest.'

Jim whispered, "Mum, your childhood and your life has had twists and turns due to my grandpa being killed by the Germans, and your mother, who never accepted her responsibilities and abandoned you. Thank God you were raised by the nuns at Marychurch. Perhaps this is your time to forgive and find your inner peace and remember the German people who suffered too."

"Thank you, Jim," I said.

I buckled my seatbelt and leaned my head back on the seat pillow and closed my eyes. My mind started drifting back to when I lived in Los Angeles, and I belonged to a writer's group that met once a week in the Jewish library at the Museum of Tolerance. My group was composed mostly of Jewish American, but they welcomed me into their group. It was education for me as a person and a writer to learn first-hand about the Holocaust. Five members of my writer's group had endured the horrors of Auschwitz during World War II.

Most of the writers were working on their autobiographies. When they read their stories, I listened with horror and deep compassion. I often cried when I was driving home from our meetings. I felt pain for the Jewish people, knowing their loss and sorrow far exceeded mine. The group touched me deep within my heart and soul.

They were humble people and were helpful to me with their critique of my book that I was writing. I will be forever grateful to them all. I learned their personal history during the Holocaust which can never be forgotten. I will never forget this courageous group of people who touched my heart forever more.

Madeline, one of the group leaders, invited us to her home during the holiday season where I shared some of their cultural food. Through all our past sorrows we could find moments of enjoying life together as one unit who shared a common denominator of the love of writing and reading history books.

I opened my eyes as the flight attendant offered me bacon, eggs, and toast for breakfast with hot coffee. I looked over at Jim and Patricia who were already eating their breakfast. I smiled and was so grateful they were on this trip with me. When I finished my breakfast, I laid my head back and enjoyed the smooth flight to Budapest.

The loudspeaker announced to prepare for landing, and I buckled my seatbelt. I looked out the window and could see the place lit up with lights that twinkled majestically as we landed at the airport. We exited the airport and took a cab to the hotel, which was downtown. The air was crisp and cold, but the holiday decorations hung up everywhere gave you that magical feeling of Christmas.

I heard Jim say, "We are here Mum".

"What a beautiful hotel," I said.

Trish said, "Maidy, the hotel is American".

We entered the hotel with our luggage and went up to our rooms. It was 7:00 PM. We decided to meet at 7:30 PM and have dinner at the hotel. I did not unpack my suitcase as we were leaving after breakfast to start the cruise. I had an overnight bag which carried the items I needed for one night.

After a delightful dinner with Jim and Patricia I decided to go back to my room and take a shower and an early night. I lay on my bed flipping TV channels back and forth until I fell asleep. I was awakened the next morning by the telephone.

It was Jimmy. "Mum, are you up?" he said on the other end of the receiver?

I answered, "I am now! I will meet you in the dining room in thirty minutes."

We left the hotel at 8:30 AM and took a twenty-minute drive by cab to the cruise ship on the Danube River, where we met a group of people checking in. I was overwhelmed with the size of my cabin and the furnishings, especially the vintage country paintings hung on the walls. Outside was a patio with two basket weave chairs. I slid open the glass doors and was faced with a morning dawn, where the air felt cool and damp. It was tranquil and peaceful. I sat down on one of the chairs and sobbed.

I loved the cabin, but I felt scared of being on my own because Jim and Patricia were on another deck. I heard a knock on the door. It was Jim coming to see if I was satisfied with my cabin. He noticed I had been crying and said,

"Mum are you alright?"

"I feel scared on this boat," I said, "and you are on another deck."

"Mum, you are on the first deck, and we are the first cabin on the second deck which is close to you." Jim answered.

I said, "Jim, the cabin is beautiful, and I will love it!"

"Mum, you take a nap, and you will feel much better, and I will make sure nothing happens to you."

I gave Jim a big hug and he left to go back to his cabin.

The following morning, I felt rested and started enjoying my seven-day cruise down the Romantic River Danube with Jim and Patricia. Here I was in the heart of Old-World Europe where empires were built and some of the world's greatest music was composed and performed by Mozart and Beethoven. I opened the patio curtains and could see bare fields lying quietly in a thin veil of morning mist. We traveled during the night, and we were in the Vienna countryside. Vienna is the capital of Austria. The boat was moving slowly and the mist was clearing. I stepped out on the patio and sat down in the wicker chair.

We cruised down the river; I could see the boughs of old trees stripped from their leaves. My eyes were fixed on a big red farmhouse with white shutters. It stood stately in the middle of the green pasture looking right back at you. When you journey along the Danube River you understand why it has inspired generations of artists, poets and musicians. I remember some of the buildings in Budapest driving from the airport. We were indulged in the passion and admiration of the historical architecture all around us.

The ship cruised at night and during the day we were able to go on land in Europe's most famous destinations including Bratislava, Vienna, Linz, Passau and Vilshofen. We ended our tour in Prague, in the Czech Republic, where we spent an extra week.

The Christmas markets were a big highlight for us. Jim. Patty and I did most of our shopping for gifts at the market as most of them were handmade by the locals. The different foods at the market were tasty and reasonably priced. I spent much of my time around the handknit shops trying on the different colorful hats and scarves. The cold weather was invigorating as you walked around listening to Christmas music. Everybody seemed happy with their families and friends.

In Vienna, we visited magnificent cathedrals, and Jim and Patricia visited the museums. We attended a Beethoven symphony in a grand majestic theater with balconies draped in red velvet, braided with gold-colored cords and tassels taking you back to the another era. Symphony Number Five was powerful and continued playing in my mind when I returned to the ship.

"Yes, I could forgive the German symphony musicians," I thought as I lay on my bed with my blinds drawn open, listening to the gentle swishing of the waves from the ship cruising down the river. We were passing through small villages of the Austrian and German countryside, and I could see flashing lights from the shores dancing across the water under the moonlit night. The music of Beethoven was simmering in my brain until I finally fell asleep.

When I awoke the next day, we were close to Passau, a short distance from Adolf Hitler's birthplace in Braunau am Inn. I drew back the curtains and saw sheets of white snow had covered my windows and glass doors. I wrapped my coat around me and stepped onto the patio and took a long deep breath. The air was crisp and cold, but the panoramic view was spectacular with all the different colored lights sparkling from the gothic homes along the river belt. Christmas lights were dancing on the river. I felt as if I had just stepped into a Christmas carol.

As I stood there at the window, I began to wonder about Hitler. What made him turn into a monster who carried such prejudice towards the Jewish people, with a desire to conquer the world, and have so many people killed and tortured?

In God We Trust

On our last night on the ship we had the privilege of dining at the Captain's table with five other guests. Sitting opposite me was a nice older couple who introduced themselves as Helga and Anton. They were from Germany.

"I am Maidy," I said, "originally from England, but my home is in America."

Anton asked, "Is this your first cruise? How do you like it?"

"I am enjoying it, especially at night, laying on the bed listening to the ripples of the river as the boat moves slowly during the night," I said. "I leave my curtains open to see the buildings on the banks of the river." I replied.

At that moment the captain welcomed us, and we all introduced ourselves and where we were from. I waved at Jim and Trish as they were sitting at the other end of the table close to the captain. When the Captain sat down the food was served. It was a seven-course dinner, but I had requested smaller portions.

As the evening progressed and wine flowed with richer conversation, I asked Anton many questions about German culture with Helga's input. I learnt about the economy and their favorite foods which were much the same as England except we did not eat sauerkraut.

Helga said, "Maidy, we have three children, two sons

and one daughter, and they are all married, and we have six grandchildren." I told them about my three children and five grandchildren who were living in America and Australia.

Anton said, "We plan to go to San Francisco next Christmas."

"If you do, please contact me and I will take you out to lunch," I said. "I will give you my phone number before we leave tonight.

They both smiled and Anton said, "Maidy, you are so kind and we will call you."

I looked at Anton and saw a charming elderly man with gray hair and a mustache, and his wife Helga, who was smiling back at me. Finally, after my third glass of wine, I mustered up enough courage to ask if they were in Germany during World War II. They both looked at me and nodded their heads.

Anton said, "Our family suffered because my father was killed, and my mother's brother was killed on D-Day."

"My two uncles were killed on D.-Day which tore my mother and father apart and affected our whole family," Helga said.

"What about you, Maidy?"

"My father's bomber plane was shot down coming back from Germany, after a bombing raid, and they were all killed."

"War did terrible things and tore up families, which left our people gutted after the war. Hitler, was a lunatic who left Germany on its knees to clean up his mess," answered Anton.

"Thank God we are in a better place and time." We reached across the table and held each other's hand.

"I am glad I met you; this was meant to be," I said. Before we parted I gave them my phone number and address in California. We hugged each other goodnight.

As I walked back to my cabin, I stopped and sat down in the lobby and watched the ship slowly move down the river. I was finally at peace and able to finish my book. Anton and Helga had listened to my story, and I had listened to them. The war had taken its toll on all of us.

Humility

As we stepped off our cruise ship in Germany, we were met with a car that we had booked to drive us to Prague. We drove through the small villages in the German countryside to reach our destination.

I sat up front with a young German student who was our driver and guide. He spoke good English, and my son and he spent most of the journey in conversation regarding the economy, education, and family traditions. Their voices faded into the background as my thoughts wandered watching the scenery outside the car window.

Morning clouds were hanging within the crispy cold air. We were driving through the German countryside. I could see the snow tip fields lying peacefully in the morning mist. There were many orchards, where trees were stripped from their fruits leaving branches hanging like coat hangers. The wind had shaken the leaves from the trees that were lined along the highway, forming a thick carpet of leaves on the side of the road.

Green pastures stretched for miles with cattle and sheep grazing in the fields. The sheep were huddled under the trees for protection from the rain which was coming down at a steady pace. I felt at home. Germany reminded me of England.

As we drove through the perfectly preserved half-timbered

village, I could see a mix of old age traditions and future thinking with their buildings after the Second World War. There were small shops and cafes with living quarters above nestled on narrow sidewalks and cobbled streets. The cottages were mostly painted white with red roofs.

I saw a river with ducks swimming and splashing with their wings. This is a land with acres of beautiful countryside. The German people were no different than the British people or any other nation. "None of us want war! We want peace!"

My mind was thinking about the war. My father dropped bombs on Germany and participated in shooting enemy planes down. This is the first time I have acknowledged what my father did to fight a war to protect his country and fellow men.

"He lost his life which tore a family apart for evermore."

Forgiveness

Dad, I have spent a lifetime trying to understand why my mother made the choices she made. She abandoned my sister Jeanette and me in an orphanage after you were killed, and left us there for ten years, finally bringing us home to a dysfunctional family. Mum and my stepfather, Andrew, were mentally and physically abusive to us.

Why Dad?

In my later years, I had a better relationship with my mother, as I began to like myself and take pride with who I had become. I was able to see how being raised by the nuns made a significant change in my life regarding my religion and morals. The nuns taught me humility, which has guided me through my job and my life.

Dad, I spent my life loving your spirit and wishing you were here in this world. Dad, I forgive you for leaving me.

Mum, you never apologized to me for your actions. You wiped my father out of your life, never wanting to talk about him. Your temper created havoc and misery in Jeanette's and my life, especially with your mental and physical abuse to us. You stood by and watched my stepfather, Andrew beat me, causing me to have a black eye and welts on my body. I had to skip school for two weeks. I have spent a lifetime trying to please you. Towards the end of your life you finally realized that I was the one who took care of you. I was the golden one."

You called my name three times before you died in the nursing home in New Zealand. "Where is my Maidy, Maidy, Maidy?" you said.

I could not come to you as I had hip surgery at that time. I had planned to come in June. But it was too late. For you Mum, I have forgiveness from my heart to enable me to let go of you and the past. I am so sorry Mum, you and Dad missed knowing my childhood and the good person I became.

My final apology is to Germany and the German people. I am sorry for the pain and suffering we shared from World War II. I am sorry if your villages and families were destroyed from the bombing of the Royal Air Force. As I drive through your country, I can see how you cherish your homes and your families.

As I listened to a conversation between my son, his wife and Hans, the driver, talking about their education system, it made me realize that after all the trials and tribulations I am finally at peace enjoying the German countryside. There is no peace without forgiveness. Forgiveness is not for others. It's a gift for you as the past cannot be changed. Accepting forgiveness is the very component in healing your body and soul.

Per Ardva Ad Astra, through adversity to the stars.

The End

Made in the USA
Las Vegas, NV
11 November 2023

80631931R00150